UNCOMPLICATED

UNCOMPLICATED

Taking the stress out of home cooking

Claire Tansey

PENGUIN

an imprint of Penguin Canada, a division of Penguin Random House Canada Limited

Canada • USA • UK • Ireland • Australia • New Zealand • India • South Africa • China

First published 2018

www.penguinrandomhouse.ca

LIBRARY AND ARCHIVES CANADA CATALOGUING IN PUBLICATION

Tansey, Claire, author
    Uncomplicated : taking the stress out of home cooking / Claire Tansey.

Issued in print and electronic formats.
ISBN 978-0-7352-3399-7 (softcover).—ISBN 978-0-7352-3400-0 (electronic)

    1. Cooking. 2. Cookbooks. I. Title.

TX714.T365 2018   641.5   C2017-907397-4
                                         C2017-907398-2

Cover and book design by Jennifer Lum
Cover images by Suech and Beck
Food styling by Melanie Stuparyk
Prop styling by Catherine Doherty

Printed and bound in China

10 9 8 7 6 5 4 3 2 1

For Michael and Thomas
There's nowhere else I'd rather be than at the dinner table with you two.

CONTENTS

BEEF, PORK AND LAMB

FISH AND SEAFOOD

VEGETARIAN

PASTA

FIVE-MINUTE VEGETABLE SIDES

UNCOMPLICATED ENTERTAINING

BAKING

Introduction

Hi, come on in. Let me tell you how I got here.

I grew up in a family that ate dinner together every single night. My mom worked full-time, and then came home and whipped up supper while my brother, sister and I bickered about who would set the table and who would walk to the train station to meet Dad on his way home from work.

At the time it didn't seem unusual—in fact all of our friends were also expected home for some kind of homemade supper. But now, as an adult, I marvel at how my mom managed it all. Of course, she didn't really have any choice. Frozen and prepared foods weren't as common then as now, and we never ate in restaurants. Like most of the other moms in our neighbourhood, she just needed to feed her family.

Those meals were simple home cooking, but they live large in my memory: little lamb chops sizzled under the broiler with baked potatoes and mint sauce from a bottle; cheese soufflé made with neon-orange Imperial cheddar served with buttered frozen peas; stir-fried beef with broccoli and cashews. We each had our assigned place at the table (I was in a direct line of my older sister's elbow), and we ate and chatted (usually) politely. My dad ate everything with immense delight, my brother told tall tales, and my sister shoved me at every opportunity.

Today, that model seems obsolete. Between long commutes, chockablock schedules, fussy eaters and special diets, who could possibly have the time, the energy and the know-how to cook supper every night, right? Now that I have a family of my own, I face the same challenges. Just getting the grocery shopping done is sometimes more than I can manage. And what about all the confusing messages about health and environment? Should I buy cage-free eggs or organic? Are avocados causing drought in California? And what the heck is chia? It's just too complicated. And yet we recognize that home cooking is good for us and benefits our families, our finances, our health and our planet. We want to come back into the kitchen—but how?

The solution is to simplify. Forget all the bells and whistles, the TV chefs, the fancy knives and gadgets. Strip away all that unnecessary noise and just cook simple, good food. That's what "uncomplicated" means to me.

I started cooking pretty young, but by the time I left home for Mount Allison University in New Brunswick, I was only cooking the basics. Then, in my third year of school, I got a job cooking in the school president's house for big parties. The pay was good, the crew was fantastic and the work was . . . well, not work at all. I was hooked.

After graduating with my bachelor of arts degree, I bought knives and chef's whites and apprenticed as a chef in fine dining.

But much as I loved the pace and energy of restaurant work, it's a young person's game, and by the time I turned thirty I transitioned out of that gruelling work and into a gentler life developing recipes for magazines and teaching cooking classes. Focusing on home cooking was much more satisfying. Much more me. I love fine cuisine, but really, I'm just hungry. Sure, I know how to fillet fish, slow-roast duck breasts and caramelize shallots, but I'd rather boil a pot of pasta and have garlic spaghetti on the table in fifteen minutes so my partner Michael, our son Thomas and I can sit together. And that's miles better for me and my family than a store-bought frozen anything.

The recipes in this book are the ones I cook at home for my family and friends—really! I'm a working mom who tries to get a tasty home-cooked meal on the table seven nights a week. That's a tall order, I know, but after more than twenty years as a food professional, I've figured out how to get to delicious with as little stress—and as few dirty dishes—as possible (though sometimes, when I don't feel like cooking, this means bread and cheese, and that's okay, too).

So on those days when you're wandering the supermarket aisles trying to think up something new and exciting to do with chicken, or trying to remember the results of the latest salmon-farming study, remember my little mantra: "Just cook it yourself. Nothing else matters." And if you're all out of dinner ideas, I've got you covered.

If you think you can't cook, you're in the right place. Because you can, and you're going to love it.

Let's get started.

THE UNCOMPLICATED KITCHEN

These recipes were developed in my home kitchen. I have a domestic gas range and an electric oven without convection. I shop at an ordinary supermarket, and all the ingredients in the book should be widely available. The only exceptions to the weekly grocery-store shop are fish and steak (see page 8). I'm not big on gadgets, but I do think it's worth it to invest in a few good-quality, long-lasting pots and pans and some other gear (see page 5). I also only use one set of measurements (mostly imperial, not metric) because I don't use metric cups and spoons in the kitchen, and the equivalency charts aren't exact. The exception here is in baking recipes, which were all tested using cups and spoons as well as gram measurements (more on page 5).

All these recipes were also tested by a crew of over a hundred volunteer home cooks in their own kitchens.

Here are some specifics about uncomplicated ingredients and equipment.

INGREDIENTS

Butter and eggs	All my recipes use salted butter. All the eggs are large.
Salt	With just two or three exceptions, all the recipes here use regular table salt. When I've called for kosher salt, it's because the recipe demands it, as using table salt would overpower or wreck the dish. Flaky sea salt, used in Grown-Up Ice Cream Sundaes (page 272), is a finishing salt, only used to garnish a dish just before serving it. I use Maldon salt. It's also wonderful on sliced steak.
Oil	I use just two types of oil in my recipes: extra-virgin olive oil and canola oil. There are lots of other delicious and versatile oils out there, but these are my two go-tos. I love canola because it is Canadian, affordable, neutral in flavour and doesn't scorch when heated. It costs about $4 for a 3 L jug, which I decant into a 1 L bottle to keep by the stove. I love the flavour of extra-virgin olive oil, but since most of the flavour dissipates during cooking, I save the good stuff for raw dishes. Use it for salads, many Mediterranean dishes and any time the oil won't be cooked.
Lemon and lime juices	Always use freshly squeezed citrus juice. The bottled stuff doesn't have the flavour, acidity or tang that fresh has, and should be avoided.
Cream and milk	When a recipe calls for whipping (35%) cream, it's crucial to the dish because it won't split when it's cooked. Otherwise, unless the recipe calls for a specific milk-fat percentage, you can use whatever you have on hand. I always have 2% milk and whipping (35%) cream in the fridge.
Yogurt	Plain yogurt is one of my favourite ingredients. That said, I think non-fat yogurt is a travesty. I use 4% or 6% plain yogurt in cooking and baking, and do not recommend anything lower than 2%. Remember that fat transmits flavour, and without it you'll need more sugar and salt.
Grated and shredded cheese	In my recipes, "shredded" refers to the stuff you buy that way in a bag. It's fine for pizza, quesadillas and topping casseroles. "Grated" is cheese you do by hand (or in a food processor). Since shredded cheese is coated with very fine granules of starch, it's not good for sauces.
Parmesan cheese	Freshly grated Parmesan cheese is one of my essential ingredients. I use Grana Padano, which costs less than Parmigiano-Reggiano but has the same oomph. Buy a large hunk and keep it wrapped in wax or parchment paper and tucked into a resealable plastic bag in the fridge. Grate it on a microplane or the small holes of a box grater as required. Save the rind to simmer with Lentil and Vegetable Soup (page 55) in the future. Although some vegetarians avoid authentic Parmesan, I surveyed my vegetarian readers and almost everyone told me they still eat Parmesan, even though it contains calf rennet. There are Parmesan-like alternatives made with non-animal rennet, if you prefer.
Leftover chicken	Several recipes in the Chicken chapter call for shredded cooked chicken because we often have leftovers from Weekday Roast Chicken (page 65), but you can easily pick up a rotisserie chicken in the supermarket or use any cooked chicken.

Spicy stuff	Cayenne, hot sauce, hot chili-garlic sauce, Sriracha and hot chili flakes are used throughout this book, mostly followed by the word "optional." I have found spice to be an even more subjective ingredient than salt, so I encourage you to add as much or as little as you think you and your fellow diners would like (although start with less. You can always add more, but it's impossible to reduce the heat after it's in the pot).
Chili powder	When these recipes were being tested by my volunteer home cooks, their questions brought me to an extremely important realization: chili powder is not chilli powder. That one extra letter has extraordinary consequences! Chili powder (one l) is a blend of spices including mild paprika, ancho chili, cumin and oregano. I use it a lot—in Fresh Vegetable Chili (page 140), Saucy Tex-Mex Black Beans (page 147) and Creamy Red Lentil Soup with Warm Spices (page 52). It is mild and fragrant and hardly spicy at all. Chilli powder (two l's), on the other hand, is the term commonly used in Indian cuisine for ground cayenne, and cannot be substituted without melting your face off. Shop wisely!
Fresh black pepper	I love pepper as long as it's freshly ground. This is another subjective ingredient, so I haven't included specific measurements for it. Just add as much or as little as you like.
Alcohol	Wine is a classic ingredient in so many cuisines, and for good reason: it brings a depth, flavour and acidity that no other ingredient can. Whenever possible, I've offered suggestions for substitutions, should you be serving children or those who don't drink. However, I do highly recommend using the real goods. There's no need to use expensive wines, but they should be drinkable—if it's awful in the bottle, it'll still be awful in the dish. Dry white vermouth is an excellent, affordable ingredient or sub for white wine (and critical to a Gin Martini, page 203). Buy a litre and keep it for up to six months in the fridge.
Vanilla	Always use real vanilla extract. The artificial stuff tastes, well, fake.
Panko crumbs and breadcrumbs	Japanese breadcrumbs, or panko, are so versatile, and one of my essential ingredients. They're much bigger than fine breadcrumbs and so get crunchy when baked. They can't usually be switched with regular store-bought or homemade fine breadcrumbs unless I've indicated that in the recipe (such as Herb and Garlic Meatloaf, page 91).
Canned whole tomatoes	The flavour and texture of whole tomatoes is far better, richer and sweeter than the ones that come pre-diced. To crush them up quickly, pour out (and save) some of the juice, then use your hand to gently crush each tomato in the can. You can also snip tomatoes into pieces (right in the can) with kitchen scissors.
Non-stick baking spray and cooking spray	I use both of these often. Cooking spray, which is flavourless oil in a spray canister, is ideal for greasing barbecue grills and roasting pans. Baking spray is even more useful. It contains a little bit of flour, so when you spray it on cake pans and muffin tins, not even a crumb of your baked goods will stick. It's also essential for bundt pans, which are close to impossible to grease properly. If you can't find it, use parchment paper to line cake pans, or grease the pan, then dust it with flour.

Digital scale

All the baked goods recipes in this book were developed and tested using cups and measuring spoons as well as gram measures. I really love using a scale for baking—it's just so much faster and tidier. Instead of measuring out 2½ cups of flour (which means filling and levelling off three different cup measures), just place a bowl on the scale and add flour.

It's also easier and less messy to measure larger amounts of sticky, wet ingredients like honey and molasses in grams.

Measurements of 2 tablespoons or less are still measured by the spoon, since most inexpensive scales aren't precise enough to know the difference between ¼ and ½ teaspoon of baking powder.

Look for a digital scale at the hardware store. I like ones that are flat, and slide easily into the cupboard. There's no need to spend more than $25.

If you use cups, don't scoop! Spoon flour or other dry ingredients like cornstarch, icing sugar and cocoa into the measuring cup, then sweep a knife across the top of the cup to level it off.

Rimmed baking sheet

This is an 11- by 17-inch metal pan with a 1-inch deep lip, often called a jellyroll pan or a half sheet pan. I have two of these, and they are the workhorses of my kitchen, used for everything from cookies to pizza to roast chicken.

Non-stick frying pans

Every kitchen needs at least one good non-stick frying pan. It's critical for easy egg cooking, and helpful in so many other ways, too. I have a small one (7 inches) and a large one (12 inches), and they both see a lot of action. You don't have to spend too much money, but take care of it (never use scouring pads or put it in the dishwasher), and once the non-stick coating starts to deteriorate, chuck it out and get a new one.

Oven-safe frying pans

This kind of pan allows you to start something on the stove, then transfer it to the oven to finish cooking. It's best to use one that does not have a non-stick coating (most don't) because it can be taken to a much higher heat and still be food-safe. A large cast-iron pan is the best option for this—inexpensive, durable and versatile.

Knives

A basic kitchen needs just three knives: a chef's knife (between 6 inches and 10 inches long), a paring knife and a serrated bread knife. Of the three, it's only worth investing in the chef's knife—the other two can be cheap and cheerful. A good chef's knife should feel comfortable in your hand, and you must be able to wrap your fingers around its handle and still be able to chop without your knuckles hitting the cutting board. Above all, keep that blade sharp; sharp knives prevent accidental cuts and make prep easier and faster.

Parchment paper

This wonder stuff is a busy cook's godsend. It's oven-safe, reusable and compostable. Use it to line baking sheets (not just for baking—roasting, too!) and cake pans. If you don't have any on hand, use aluminum foil sprayed with non-stick cooking spray (or, for baked goods, use non-stick baking spray). Wax paper is not a substitute, since it melts.

HOW TO USE THESE RECIPES

For many years I kept a sharp eye on the nutritional values and portion sizes of any recipe I developed. I made sure the sodium, calories and saturated fats weren't too high and that the fibre was high enough. And yet, even though I know all the standard daily recommendations by heart, I still get confused by it all. The word "healthy" these days means something different to everyone, and with food and nutrition science progressing quickly, it's hard to keep track of what's good for me and what isn't. New research today, for example, questions whether saturated fats and sodium are really as bad as we previously thought. Who knows where we'll be in five or ten years.

My solution in life is the one I bring to this book: forget the numbers and just cook it yourself. I'm certain that when I cook real food, nothing else matters. Instead, I focus on enjoying the process of cooking, and doubly enjoying the time I get to spend with friends and family when there's a home-cooked meal on the table. That's as healthy as I strive to be.

I have included with my recipes a number of elements that I hope home cooks find useful:

Prep Time This is roughly how much active cooking time you'll need to get the recipe going. This includes chopping, measuring, stirring and, yes, even the time it takes to locate the brown sugar at the back of the pantry.

Ready In After years in the business of reading, writing and editing recipes, I find this is the time measurement that's the most useful to me when planning a meal. It includes prep and cooking time, as well as cooling or standing time. I start the timer when I walk into the kitchen and stop it when I'm putting my fork in my mouth.

For quick reference, you'll find these designations as they pertain to each recipe:

Make ahead The entire recipe, or parts of it, can be made ahead and reheated or completed without affecting the quality of the finished dish.

Batch cooking The dish can be multiplied and frozen, then reheated.

Slow cooker The recipe can be made in an electric slow cooker (with slight modifications).

Switch it up Easy variations you can choose to use. All variations have been tested.

UNCOMPLICATED SHOPPING

The hardest part of cooking is shopping. It is the most underrated, unrecognized cooking skill, and I wish there were as many helpful videos on Facebook about shopping as there are about making dinner.

I know making a weekly meal plan and accompanying grocery list would be helpful, of course, but I've never been able to do it. Instead, I keep the pantry well stocked and just pop out every few days for fresh ingredients. But I know not everyone lives around the corner from a grocery store, so I recommend creating, and memorizing (or keeping on your phone), a list of ingredients you always need to have on hand and simply supplementing with once-a-week necessities.

Here are my everyday kitchen staples, which are the backbone of all the recipes in this book. From these you can whip up any number of meals. Tweak the list to adapt to your household's specific likes and wants.

Essentials: Buy these once a week.

Two fresh vegetables (such as broccoli and bok choy); carrots; apples; garlic; lemons or limes; parsley, cilantro or thyme; bread; milk; cream; yogurt; Cheddar cheese; feta cheese; eggs; butter

Basics: These last longer than a week. Once you run out, restock immediately.

The Pantry

- Onions; ginger
- Flour (all-purpose, and whole wheat if you use it often); baking soda and baking powder; granulated sugar; brown sugar; vanilla; chocolate chips
- Salt; whole peppercorns; cayenne; chili powder; cinnamon; ground coriander; ground cumin; curry powder; garlic powder; ground ginger; onion powder; dried thyme
- Canola oil; extra-virgin olive oil; soy sauce; red wine vinegar; coconut milk
- Pasta; basmati rice
- Canned black beans or chickpeas; dried lentils or split peas
- Canned plum tomatoes; tomato paste; tuna

The Fridge

- Parmesan cheese; mayonnaise; Dijon mustard; maple syrup; Thai and Indian curry pastes; miso paste; sesame oil; dry (white) vermouth

The Freezer

- Frozen peas, corn or edamame; tortillas; berries

Find a good butcher, and buy good meat.

Almost everything that makes meat delicious happens before you even walk into the store. Meat that is raised, butchered, aged and packaged with care and attention simply tastes better, and that's why I recommend taking some time to find it.

It's worth it to find a source for meat where you can speak with a butcher in person, and whose offerings are not all pre-packaged. Not only will the butcher usually be able to tell you all kinds of helpful information about the meat, but they will also be able to spatchcock a chicken (page 228) or cut a two-inch rib-eye (page 88) for you.

Some supermarkets still have a butcher on staff and a good meat counter. It's worth starting there. Buy and cook something like a steak or whole chicken and decide how you enjoyed the experience and flavours.

You can also start by asking cooks or food lovers you trust to recommend their favourite places, or by doing an internet search for the best independent butchers in your area. (If you come up with nothing, or if you live in a rural area, research small producers that do a direct delivery of frozen meat.)

Visit the recommended shops and take a good look around. Good butcher shops have some meat on display with much more available in the back, as well as a few things pre-packaged in the display case, and a full freezer of goodies. Strike up a conversation with a staff person. They should be able to tell you the specific farms from which the shop sources its meat.

The final test is in the eating. Buy some bacon, a chicken, a pork roast or steak and serve it fairly plainly. If its flavour doesn't knock your socks off, you might want to try the next shop on your list.

Shopping at an independent butcher isn't usually cheaper than the supermarket, but I find that we eat less steak and pork because we savour each bite much more, and we tend to use up every scrap of our chickens because they taste so much better.

As a side note, organic meat isn't necessarily better. Many great butchers sell exceptional products from smaller farms who can't afford to or choose not to get an organic certification. For me, it's all about the flavour.

Finally, I try not to buy anything pre-packaged, except ground meat, because the meat's surface gets too soggy, making it difficult to brown nicely.

Source good fish and seafood.

Most of the butcher advice applies to fish stores, too, although some of the best fish counters I've seen are in supermarkets with a discerning clientele and high turnover.

A great fish shop or counter should not smell like fish. The fish on display should look firm, clear and clean. Staff should be able to fillet or skin any fish for you.

It's also worth remembering that frozen and canned fish are often fresher than what's on display in the fish counter, since frozen and canned products are packed and processed at sea or right at the shore.

Regardless of where you shop, try not to buy pre-marinated fish or meat. I guarantee you it's not the shop's freshest product, and you can add better flavour with a simple squeeze of lemon and some salt.

Breakfast and Brunch

Weekday Pancakes

Makes 9 to 12 pancakes • Make ahead

Prep Time 10 minutes or less
Ready In 15 to 20 minutes

2 cups (310 g) whole wheat flour

2 tablespoons granulated sugar (optional)

2 teaspoons ground flaxseed (optional)

1½ teaspoons baking powder

1 teaspoon baking soda

1 teaspoon salt

½ teaspoon cinnamon (optional)

2 eggs

1½ cups milk

½ cup plain yogurt

½ teaspoon pure vanilla extract (optional)

2 tablespoons butter, melted, or canola oil

I created this recipe to save my own sanity. My son, Thomas, loves having pancakes for breakfast, but to save precious sleeping-in time (and lessen my parental guilt) I had to rework my classic buttery pancake recipe. Whole wheat flour, ground flaxseed and optional sugar make these pancakes healthier, and I often make the dry mix ahead of time, which means a plate of fresh pancakes is less than 10 minutes away. Serve these with Secretly Green Smoothies (page 34) for a satisfying start to a weekday, or for a weekend breakfast, add Roasted Maple-Cayenne Bacon (page 27).

1. Whisk the flour with the sugar (if using), flaxseed (if using), baking powder, baking soda, salt and cinnamon (if using) in a large bowl. In a separate bowl, whisk the eggs with the milk, yogurt and vanilla, if using. Whisk in the melted butter. Pour the egg mixture into the flour mixture and stir with a rubber spatula until it's barely combined. There should still be a few streaks of flour in the batter.

2. Heat a large non-stick frying pan or flat griddle over medium heat. Let it get it hot, then spray or wipe the pan with a little butter or canola oil. Use about ⅓ cup batter per pancake. Once lots of little bubbles appear on the uncooked side, flip the pancakes and cook until the golden side (now facing up) loses its shininess and appears matte. Do not flip pancakes more than once and never press down on pancakes while they're cooking.

3. Serve immediately or transfer in a single layer to a rack set over a baking sheet and keep warm in a 200°F oven.

Make ahead Mix the dry ingredients together and store in an airtight container at room temperature for up to 2 weeks.

Switch it up After pouring batter into the pan, you can sprinkle each pancake with fresh blueberries or mini chocolate chips. This method is better than mixing the extras right into the batter—this way each pancake gets the same number of add-ins.

Buttermilk Waffles

Makes 8 to 12 waffles • Make ahead

I have an old waffle iron that someone gave me years ago. It only makes two waffles at a time and it's nearly impossible to clean properly, but it sees a lot of action in my kitchen. Waffles are great for breakfast, but equally wonderful as the bread for sandwiches or as a base for something like Mushrooms on Toast (page 33). Buttermilk is the key ingredient here; it usually only comes in 1 litre cartons but lasts well over a week in the fridge (and freezes well) so you can have these on two consecutive weekends. Although it's possible to mimic buttermilk by adding vinegar to regular milk, these waffles don't come out nearly as fluffy and delicious.

···

1. Preheat the waffle iron.

2. Stir the flour with the sugar, baking powder, baking soda and salt in a medium bowl. In a separate medium bowl, whisk the eggs, then whisk in the buttermilk and melted butter. Add the wet mixture to the dry mixture and stir until just combined. Batter should be thick (it will spread out in the pan).

3. Spray the waffle iron lightly with non-stick cooking spray. Cook waffles in batches, using about ⅓ cup of batter per waffle, or follow your waffle iron's instructions.

4. Serve right away or transfer to a rack set over a baking sheet and keep warm in a 200°F oven.

Make ahead Cool the waffles completely on a rack, then freeze for up to 2 weeks in a resealable plastic bag. Reheat from frozen on low in the toaster.

Switch it up Substitute whole wheat flour for up to half the all-purpose flour and omit the sugar. After adding the melted butter to the egg mixture, stir in ½ cup grated old Cheddar and ¼ teaspoon dried thyme. Serve these savoury cheese waffles topped with a fried egg.

Prep Time 10 minutes
Ready In 15 minutes or less

2 cups (300 g) all-purpose flour

¼ cup (50 g) granulated sugar

2 teaspoons baking powder

1 teaspoon baking soda

½ teaspoon salt

2 eggs

2 cups buttermilk, well shaken before measuring

¼ cup butter, melted, or canola oil

French Toast with Swiss Cheese and Apples

Serves 4 • Make ahead

I made this for the first time at the end of a long recipe-testing day. I was tired, full from tasting multiple dishes and anxious to not be around food for a while (it happens occasionally). I expected to make this, have one taste, pop the leftovers into the fridge and close up the kitchen for the day. That's not exactly what happened. After one bite I couldn't stop. This golden, crisp but fluffy French toast with melty cheese and caramelized apples, all drizzled in smoky maple syrup, knocked my socks off.

French toast is a genius way to use up stale bread, but it doesn't turn out well with whole wheat or multigrain bread; I don't know exactly why, but it's just not right. A dense white bread, like artisanal Italian, sourdough or challah, is ideal. It really doesn't matter what kind of cream or milk you add—in fact it can be a good way to use up a little bit of this and that—so just use whatever you have in the fridge. Use firm apples, such as Granny Smith or Gala, and no need to peel them—enjoy the added fibre.

....

1. Whisk the eggs, milk, 1 tablespoon of the sugar and salt in a large shallow dish (such as a 9- x 13-inch baking dish). Add the bread, press it down and leave it to soak for at least 15 minutes but up to 2 hours.

2. Close to serving time, melt the butter in a large non-stick frying pan over medium heat. Add the apples and the remaining 1 tablespoon sugar. Cook, stirring often, 6 to 9 minutes or until apples are very soft and lightly golden. Transfer to a bowl and cover to keep warm.

3. Wipe out the pan with damp paper towels and return to medium heat. Add the canola oil. Remove a slice of bread from the egg mixture, letting a little of the excess drip off, and carefully place in the pan. Repeat with more bread until the pan is full but there is still a little space around each slice (if your pan isn't big enough, do this in batches). Cook 3 minutes or until the bottom is golden. Flip, reduce heat to low and cook another 3 minutes. Place 1 or 2 slices of cheese on each slice of bread and cook another 1 to 2 minutes or until the cheese melts a bit.

4. Serve immediately, topped with warm apple mixture and drizzled with maple syrup.

Prep Time 15 minutes
Ready In a little over ½ hour

4 eggs

1 cup 2% milk or whipping (35%) cream

2 tablespoons granulated sugar, divided

¼ teaspoon salt

4 large slices of bread (1 to 1½ inches thick), at least a day old

2 tablespoons butter

2 large firm apples, cored and thinly sliced

2 teaspoons canola oil

4 to 8 thin slices Swiss cheese

Pure maple syrup, for serving

Make ahead Cook the French toast but stop before adding the cheese. Keep refrigerated for up to 1 day. Reheat in a frying pan over medium-low heat for a few minutes, then place the cheese on top and continue with the recipe. The apple mixture can be made up to a day in advance as well; store it in the fridge and reheat in the microwave or on the stove before serving.

Scrambled Eggs for a Crowd

Serves 8 • Make ahead

Prep Time 5 minutes
Ready In about 30 minutes

¼ cup butter

16 eggs

½ teaspoon salt

¼ cup whipping (35%) cream

¼ cup chopped fresh chives, parsley or tarragon

Fresh black pepper

Brunch is an appealing meal to host. There's something about the daylight that removes much of the stress of entertaining. Eggs are a natural choice, but that said, poaching or frying them for a group of people can be stressful. Instead, whisk up a pan of slowly cooked, creamy scrambled eggs. There's no panic here, everyone loves them, and you can whisk intermittently while buttering an endless stack of toast and making the coffee. These eggs are more like creamy custard than your typical flash-cooked, super-dry diner eggs, and they go perfectly on thin slices of toast. For an unforgettable brunch, serve them with smoked salmon and Lemony Broiled Asparagus (page 182) on the side, and maybe a pan of Blueberry-Bran Muffin Cake (page 37) too.

1. Melt the butter in a large non-stick frying pan over low heat.

2. Add the eggs (you can crack them right into the pan) and salt, then whisk them gently until the whites and yolks combine. Whisk every 30 seconds at first, then continue to whisk every minute or so, occasionally scraping the sides and bottom of the pan with a silicone or rubber spatula. (This takes a while, but don't fret. Make some toast, set the table, sip your coffee.) After 6 or 8 minutes the eggs will be firming up and forming lumps. They are done when you see the bottom of the pan after you whisk.

3. Drizzle the cream all over the top of the eggs and whisk it into the eggs. Remove from the heat, and sprinkle with herbs and lots of pepper. Serve immediately.

Make ahead You can let the eggs sit, off the heat, for up to 10 minutes. It's not much, but sometimes that's all you need to get a few other things finished, like setting the table or broiling some asparagus. Cover the pan loosely with a lid or piece of foil until ready to serve.

Cheese Omelette

Serves 1

All of my culinary heroes, from Julia Child to Elizabeth David, claim that omelettes are the ultimate easy meal for one. Sophisticated enough to feel special, and yet fast enough to not be any bother, an omelette is lovely for breakfast, with toast on the side, or with a salad and a glass of wine for dinner.

Omelettes are more about technique than ingredients. You have to start with the right gear: a 7-inch non-stick frying pan in tip-top shape and a silicone or rubber spatula. It's also important to have all the ingredients ready to go before heating the pan. Go easy on the toppings: adding an abundance of toppings usually leads to overcooked eggs and the whole thing becoming a sloppy mess. Serve this with Roasted Maple-Cayenne Bacon (page 27) for breakfast, or with Supper Salad (page 47) for dinner.

Prep Time less than 5 minutes
Ready In about 5 minutes

1 teaspoon butter

2 eggs

⅛ teaspoon salt

⅓ cup grated old Cheddar cheese

1 tablespoon finely chopped fresh chives or green onion (optional)

Fresh black pepper

1. Melt the butter in a 7-inch non-stick frying pan over medium heat.

2. While it's melting, whisk the eggs and salt in a small bowl with a fork. They should be well blended but not frothy. Use a silicone or rubber spatula to spread the butter so it covers the pan. Pour in the eggs and wait 30 seconds or so, until the bottom bit of the omelette firms up. Tilt the pan and use the spatula to tuck in the edges of the omelette—just an inch or so—so runny egg from on top runs towards the outside edge of the pan. Wiggle the pan so any remaining runny parts meet with cooked parts. Cook until the egg is mostly set but still moist.

3. Sprinkle cheese and chives (if using) evenly over the omelette and cook another 30 seconds or until the cheese is mostly melted. Season with pepper.

4. Pick up the pan and let half of the omelette slowly slide out onto a plate (you might need to encourage it with the spatula); then use the pan to flop the top half over the bottom half, leaving you with a half-moon omelette. Serve immediately.

Tip When feeding more than just yourself, I'm a proponent of making omelettes one at a time, instead of trying to divide a big, melting, cheesy mass into portions. Make them for others first, wiping out the pan with paper towels in between each omelette, and serve yourself last.

Switch it up Sprinkle the omelette with 2 tablespoons of any cooked ingredient, such as sautéed mushrooms, steamed and squeezed spinach, grilled peppers, cooked sausage or bacon just before adding the cheese.

Bubble and Squeak

Serves 2 to 4

Prep Time 5 minutes
Ready In about 10 minutes

1½ cups leftover mashed potatoes

2 green onions, finely chopped

⅛ teaspoon curry powder

Fresh black pepper

1 tablespoon butter

4 eggs

Salt

Switch it up Substitute up to half of the potatoes with any leftover cooked vegetables (such as sweet potatoes, carrots, green beans, turkey stuffing or peas). Instead of a poached egg, top with a little smoked salmon or fried black pudding.

Although I love big, raucous dinner parties, I invariably enjoy the food more the day after the event. After the fuss of hosting, a quiet meal of leftovers gives me more time to savour the flavours. But the day after that, any leftovers still in the fridge are a burden. The solution is this British classic. It does depend on there being some mashed potatoes in the fridge, but that's reason enough to add an extra spud or two to the pot in the first place. Serve this with a batch of Roasted Maple-Cayenne Bacon (page 27).

1. Stir the potatoes with the green onions and curry powder in a medium bowl. Season with pepper. Shape into 4 patties.

2. Melt the butter in a large non-stick frying pan over medium heat. Add the patties and cook 2 to 4 minutes (without moving the patties) or until deeply golden and a little bit crispy on the bottom and hot throughout. With a thin spatula, flip the patties, and cook another 2 minutes. Remove the pan from the heat, but leave the patties in the pan to stay warm until the eggs are ready.

3. Meanwhile, fill a wide medium frying pan or very shallow pot three-quarters full with water. Bring to a gentle simmer over medium heat. Crack one egg into a saucer or small bowl. Place the edge of the saucer as close to the simmering water as you can get (without burning yourself!) and slip the egg into the water very gently. The egg whites will "feather" or spread out in the pan; don't worry and also, do not touch. Repeat with the remaining eggs. After 2 minutes at a low simmer, gently ease a slotted spoon under each egg, getting right between it and the pan. Now the egg will float to the top of the water. Cook another 30 seconds to 2 minutes, depending on how runny you want the yolk.

4. Use the slotted spoon to lift each egg out of the water, then rest the spoon on a little stack of paper towels to wick away any water. Transfer one egg to one bubble and squeak patty and sprinkle with salt and pepper. Serve immediately.

Tip Depending on how soft the original mashed potatoes were, these patties will be less or more easy to flip. Regardless, when the time comes, slip a thin spatula under the patty in one swift movement. You only get one chance, so don't be shy, or the patty will break apart. Still delicious, just not as pretty.

Roasted Maple-Cayenne Bacon

Serves 4

Cooking bacon in the oven is one of my favourite kitchen de-stressors. In a frying pan bacon requires frequent tending-to, and even then it's impossible to get all the bacon flat, and parts of each slice end up over- or under-cooked. Not good. Meanwhile the popping and splattering of bacon fat not only makes a mess of the cooktop but almost always injures some unsuspecting person passing by the stove. Roasted bacon, by contrast, always comes out perfectly flat and crisp, and no one gets hurt. The cayenne here is optional, but those who like a bit of kick go wild for the spicy-sweet combo; if children are present, omit the cayenne on their bacon. Serve this with Weekday Pancakes (page 14), Buttermilk Waffles (page 17), Scrambled Eggs for a Crowd (page 20) or Bubble and Squeak (page 24).

Prep Time 5 minutes
Ready In about 20 minutes

13 ounces (375 g) thick-cut bacon (about 12 slices)

2 tablespoons pure maple syrup

¼ teaspoon cayenne

1. Preheat the oven to 400°F. Line a rimmed baking sheet with parchment paper.

2. Spread out the bacon in a single layer on the parchment. You can squeeze the slices right up against each other and use every inch of space on the baking sheet. Brush the tops of the bacon with maple syrup, then sprinkle with cayenne.

3. Roast 15 to 20 minutes or until evenly crispy, turning the slices over halfway through. Rest briefly on paper towels to soak up a little of the grease. Serve immediately.

Switch it up Try different spices in place of or in addition to cayenne. Ground coriander, fennel, cinnamon, nutmeg, curry powder and ginger would each bring something interesting to the flavours.

Everyday Granola

Makes 6 cups • Make ahead • Batch cooking

Prep Time 10 minutes
Ready In about 1½ hours

3 cups (300 g) large-flake oats

1 cup (100 g) raw pecan or walnut halves

¾ cup (120 g) raw pepitas

½ cup (70 g) raw sunflower seeds

¼ cup (40 g) whole flax seeds

¾ teaspoon cinnamon

½ teaspoon salt

½ cup canola oil

½ cup (160 g) pure maple syrup or liquid honey

1 teaspoon pure vanilla extract (optional)

¾ cup (125 g) dried fruit, chopped if large, such as apricots or prunes

In my battered yet beloved recipe notebook, where I've been keeping track of borrowed and invented recipes for over twenty years, there are several entries for granola. Clearly it's a thing for me, but I had never found *the one*. After years of experimenting with granolas that were too sticky, too oily, too dry and just not good enough, I finally hit on this one. It's so easy and turns out crisp and sweet but not gooey (just right!). It's wonderful with plain yogurt, milk or almond milk, but I also pack it as is for an on-the-go snack. This is also my go-to hostess gift, packed into a mason jar and tied with a little ribbon. I've included weights here because I find weighing speeds up the prep.

....

1. Preheat the oven to 350°F. Line a rimmed baking sheet with parchment paper.

2. Stir the oats with the pecans, pepitas, sunflower seeds, flax seeds, cinnamon and salt in a large bowl. In a medium bowl, whisk the canola oil with the maple syrup (if using honey, microwave for 30 seconds if it's too solid to whisk) and vanilla (if using), then pour it over the oat mixture. Stir until all the oat flakes are coated.

3. Tip the mixture onto the prepared pan and spread it into a thin, even layer. Bake 30 to 40 minutes, giving it a really good stir every 10 or 15 minutes. The granola should be golden and toasty, but not too dark brown. Keep a close eye on it during the last 10 minutes, as it can over-toast quickly.

4. Let it cool on the baking sheet, then stir in the dried fruit. Store it in an airtight container at room temperature for up to 10 days.

Make ahead Freeze granola, minus the dried fruit, in resealable plastic bags for up to 3 months. Add the fruit when you serve it.

Batch cooking This recipe doubles well. Use two pans instead of one and switch them around in the oven halfway through baking.

Switch it up For a different but equally yummy variation, add ¼ teaspoon each of ground cardamom, ground ginger and nutmeg, and use almond extract in place of the vanilla.

Instant Bircher Muesli

Serves 2

Prep Time 5 minutes or less
Ready In about 20 minutes

¾ cup quick oats

¾ cup unsweetened
apple juice

⅛ teaspoon cinnamon or
cardamom

⅛ teaspoon salt

1 ripe but crisp pear (such
as Bosc or Asian), cubed

¼ cup chopped toasted
walnuts or almonds

2 tablespoons Power Seeds
(see page 44; optional)

Bircher muesli, typically a mix of uncooked large-flake oats soaked overnight with milk and apples, appears every now and then on breakfast menus, and it always sounds so appealing and healthy. I'm rarely organized enough to make something in the evening for the next morning, and when I am, my breakfast cravings often change between the evening stir-up and the breakfast table. This "instant" version is my solution: Use quick oats, and soak them only for a few minutes (while brewing coffee or having a shower). The oats become tender quickly, and, best of all, using apple juice instead of the traditional milk makes this taste like hearty applesauce. Crisp fall pears are one of my favourite toppings, but any seasonal fruit, like berries, apples or peaches, works well.

· ·

1. Stir together the oats, apple juice, cinnamon and salt in a medium bowl, then set aside for about 15 minutes.

2. Stir well, then stir in pear and walnuts. Top with Power Seeds (if using).

Switch it up Instead of the nuts (or in addition to—there are no rules), swirl in a big spoonful of almond butter or plain Balkan-style yogurt after the muesli soaks.

Mushrooms on Toast

Serves 2

I'm usually all about an omelette at breakfast, but when I'm tired of eggs, this is my go-to dish. It feels heartier than avocado toast or toast with peanut butter, perhaps because it's hot. It also happily accepts a poached egg (see page 24), sliced leftover steak or just a big dollop of ricotta to make it an even more substantial breakfast. The inspiration for this came from my travels in England, where mushrooms are always part of a "full English" breakfast. A proper full English—eggs, sausages, bacon, baked beans, black pudding, fried bread, broiled mushrooms and tomatoes—is far too much work for a weekday, but this easy dish is not.

· ·

1. Quarter the mushrooms (you should have about 3 cups). Melt the butter in a medium non-stick frying pan over medium-high heat. Add mushrooms and cook, without stirring, 2 minutes, then cook, stirring occasionally, 3 more minutes or until the mushrooms are golden and tender and the pan is quite dry. Reduce heat to low and stir in green onions and salt. Cook 1 minute, then stir in lemon juice and parsley.

2. Remove from the heat and stir in the cream. Season with pepper. Toast the bread, then top with mushroom mixture. Serve immediately.

Tip It's a myth that mushrooms shouldn't be washed. Food scientists have proven that mushrooms do not absorb water when they are cleaned in water. I drop mine into a large bowl, fill it with enough water so the mushrooms float, swish them around a bit, then leave them for a few minutes. The dirt will drop to the bottom of the bowl and you can just lift the mushrooms out. Mushrooms should be patted dry before being sautéed or they won't get quite so golden.

Prep Time less than
15 minutes
Ready In about 20 minutes

8 ounces (225 g) button mushrooms

1 tablespoon butter

2 green onions, finely chopped

⅛ teaspoon salt

1 tablespoon fresh lemon juice

2 tablespoons chopped fresh parsley

2 tablespoons whipping (35%) cream

Fresh black pepper

2 thick slices of bread

Secretly Green Smoothie

Serves 2

Prep Time less than 5 minutes
Ready In 5 minutes or less

1 ripe banana

1 cup frozen raspberries
(or your favourite berries)

1 cup plain Greek yogurt

½ cup frozen chopped
kale stems

1 cup cold water or 2% milk

This recipe sort of started out as a kale salad. A few years ago I went through a phase of eating kale salads a couple of times a week, and since I trim out and toss the thick ribs of kale leaves, there was a ton of waste every time. I started coarsely chopping and freezing the ribs with the idea of one day adding them to a pot roast or something. Of course that never happened, but I did add a few to a smoothie one morning and discovered that the frozen kale disintegrates and essentially disappears with the power of a high-speed blender. Meanwhile the banana and berries mask the kale flavour. This recipe makes about 3 cups of smoothie, perfect for an on-the-go breakfast for two. It's also lovely alongside my Weekday Pancakes (page 14).

1. Combine banana, berries, yogurt, kale and water in a high-speed blender and purée until smooth. Serve immediately.

Tip I find Greek yogurt too pasty to eat on its own, but it's perfect here and adds a welcome protein boost. This isn't an overly sweet smoothie, so use vanilla yogurt if you prefer yours on the sweeter side.

Switch it up No frozen kale? Add half a ripe avocado instead and increase the water to 1½ cups.

Blueberry-Bran Muffin Cake

Makes one 8-inch square cake • Serves 9 • Make ahead

I've always loved coffee-shop raisin bran muffins, and while I was pregnant I craved them every day at 10 a.m. sharp. But since most store-bought muffins are just cakes in disguise that pack more fat, sugar and calories than a fast-food burger, I tried to reinvent them at home. It took many batches to get them perfectly moist, sweet and healthful, but I got there. Along the way, I also switched wild blueberries for raisins and poured the batter into one square dish instead of muffin tins. Success! I think this muffin cake is even more moist (but less unpleasantly greasy) than the coffee-shop version. Plus, there isn't enough fat or sugar here to make anyone too angry, and the fibre can't be beat. Serve with Secretly Green Smoothies (page 34) for a healthy breakfast.

....

1. Preheat the oven to 375°F. Grease an 8-inch square baking dish with non-stick baking spray (see page 4).

2. Stir the wheat bran with the flour, baking powder, baking soda, salt and cinnamon in a large bowl. In a medium bowl, whisk the eggs a little, then whisk in the melted butter, brown sugar and molasses. Next whisk in the milk.

3. Pour the wet mixture into the flour mixture and fold the two together with a rubber spatula. Just before they are fully incorporated, fold in the blueberries. Immediately scrape into the prepared pan.

4. Bake 30 minutes or until springy when pressed and a cake tester inserted into the centre comes out clean. Let cool on a rack. Serve warm or at room temperature.

Tip 1. Wheat bran is the fibrous exterior of wheat berries. It's essentially pure fibre, and it contributes texture, nutty flavour and nutrition. Look for it near the oatmeal in the cereal aisle, or at health food stores. Just like whole wheat flour, it can go rancid at room temperature, so store it in the freezer.
2. When using frozen blueberries in baking recipes, don't thaw them first, or they'll bleed into the batter. Instead, take them out of the freezer just before you add them to the mix. Wild blueberries are much smaller than cultivated ones, and so disperse more evenly in the batter and don't create holes in the cake once it's cooked.

Prep Time 15 minutes
Ready In about 45 minutes

1½ cups (75 g) wheat bran

1 cup (150 g) all-purpose flour

1½ teaspoons baking powder

½ teaspoon baking soda

½ teaspoon salt

¼ teaspoon cinnamon

2 eggs

¼ cup (60 g) butter, melted

¼ cup (60 g) packed brown sugar

¼ cup (90 g) fancy molasses

1 cup 2% milk

1 cup (155 g) fresh or frozen wild blueberries

Make ahead Bake the cake and let cool completely. Keep it in the baking pan, covered tightly with plastic wrap at room temperature, for up to 3 days, or take it out of the pan, wrap in foil, then freeze in a large resealable plastic bag for up to 2 weeks. Thaw, still wrapped, at room temperature.

Main Course Salads and Soups

Salade Niçoise

Serves 4 • Make ahead

Prep Time 30 minutes
Ready In about 40 minutes

6 medium red-skinned
potatoes, cut in half

8 ounces (225 g) green or
yellow beans, stem ends
trimmed

4 eggs

1 head Boston lettuce

8 ounces (225 g) cherry
tomatoes, cut in half
(about 2 cups)

4 cans (3 ounces/80 g each)
olive-oil-packed tuna

French Vinaigrette (see
page 47)

4 anchovy fillets (optional)

When it comes to main-course salads, Niçoise is the original and still champion. This dreamy collection of ingredients, prettily arranged on a plate and drizzled with tangy dressing, is sophisticated enough for company, and I often serve it for a summer dinner party. Since it's also made in advance, it's ideal for entertaining. It does take a little strategic timing, which I've included here, but if you have leftover cooked potatoes or green beans, by all means use them. You can also switch up many of the ingredients—try using smoked salmon instead of tuna, asparagus instead of beans, or sliced baguette instead of potatoes—depending on what's in season (or in the fridge).

....

1. Bring a large pot of salted water to a boil. Prepare a large bowl of ice and water.

2. Add the potatoes to the boiling water and cook 15 minutes or until tender. Remove potatoes with a slotted spoon (don't drain the water) and place them on a plate to cool.

3. Now add the beans to the boiling water and cook 3 to 6 minutes or until just tender-crisp. Immediately transfer the beans to the ice-water bath.

4. Use a slotted spoon to lower the eggs into the boiling water. Once the water returns to a boil, reduce heat and boil gently 5 minutes for just slightly runny eggs or 8 minutes for fully firm eggs. Transfer the eggs to the ice-water bath. Once cooled, drain the eggs and beans and reserve.

5. Just before serving, cut the potatoes into bite-sized pieces. Peel the eggs and cut them in half. Arrange lettuce, tomatoes, beans, potatoes and eggs on 4 plates. Drain tuna and place one can's worth on each plate. Drizzle everything with just a little French Vinaigrette. Tuck one anchovy (if using) into each salad.

6. Serve additional vinaigrette in a small pitcher alongside.

Tip Tuna packed in olive oil is immeasurably more flavourful and tender than the water-packed stuff. Look for brands imported from Italy. I drain off a little of the oil, but not too much.

Make ahead The potatoes, eggs and beans can all be cooked up to 1 day in advance. Keep refrigerated, but let come to room temperature before using.

Green Goddess Salad

Serves 4 • Make ahead

As much as I love the flavour of fresh herbs, the large bunches they are sold in really annoys me. It seems inevitable that at the end of making a recipe I'll have half a bunch of a tender green herb like tarragon left over. I often make this delicious dressing to use it up and preserve it for the rest of the week. It's inspired by the classic green goddess dressing, but simplified, since the classic calls for at least three herbs, watercress, anchovies and raw eggs. This easy version is creamy and beautifully pale green—perfect for drizzling over a salad of a variety of green things. Use an equal amount of fresh basil, cilantro, chives, chervil or dill in place of the parsley and/or tarragon and the dressing will be quite different but still tasty.

....

1. To make the Green Goddess Dressing, combine parsley, tarragon, mayonnaise, buttermilk, lemon juice, Worcestershire sauce, garlic and salt in a small blender. Whirl until smooth.

2. Divide the greens among 4 wide, shallow bowls. Top with celery, avocado and edamame. Drizzle with Green Goddess Dressing. Garnish with seaweed and serve.

Tip No buttermilk? Use 3 tablespoons plain yogurt mixed with 1 tablespoon water.

Make ahead This dressing lasts well in the fridge for up to 3 days. It does get more garlicky as it sits, but it's still delicious.

Switch it up Replace the buttermilk with Greek yogurt or sour cream and serve the dressing as a dip for chips and veggies.

Prep Time 25 minutes or less
Ready In about 25 minutes

Green Goddess Dressing

¼ cup packed fresh parsley leaves

¼ cup packed fresh tarragon leaves

¼ cup mayonnaise

¼ cup buttermilk, shaken before measuring

1 tablespoon fresh lemon juice

1 teaspoon Worcestershire sauce

1 very small clove garlic, peeled

¼ teaspoon salt

Salad

8 cups mixed greens

4 stalks celery, sliced

1 avocado, pitted and cubed

1 cup frozen shelled edamame, thawed

1 package (0.18 ounce/5 g) seaweed snacks, snipped into strips

Miso Greens with Chickpeas and Power Seeds

Serves 4 • Make ahead • Batch cooking

Prep Time 15 minutes
Ready In 15 minutes, if you toast the seeds ahead of time

Power Seeds

¼ cup whole flax seeds

¼ cup pepitas

¼ cup sunflower seeds

2 tablespoons sesame seeds

2 tablespoons poppy seeds

Miso Dressing

½ cup water

¼ cup miso paste (see Tip)

3 tablespoons apple cider vinegar

1 teaspoon Dijon mustard

1 very small clove garlic

⅓ cup canola oil

Salad

8 cups baby spinach

1 small radicchio, torn

1 can (19 ounces/540 mL) chickpeas, drained and rinsed

1 English cucumber, sliced

1 avocado, pitted and sliced

Although I eat green salad almost every day, I really only use two different dressings. Classic French Vinaigrette (see page 47) is my go-to, but several times a year I crave the intense richness of this Miso Dressing. It's spectacular on greens, but equally good drizzled on baked tofu, steamed broccoli or leftover chicken. This toasted seed mixture is another pantry staple that I always have on hand to use in salads, on yogurt or just by the handful for a protein- and nutrient-packed snack. It's also wonderful on oatmeal or Instant Bircher Muesli (page 30).

1. Preheat the oven to 375°F.

2. To make the Power Seeds, combine the flax seeds, pepitas, sunflower seeds, sesame seeds and poppy seeds on a rimmed baking sheet. Roast, stirring once, 4 to 8 minutes or until lightly toasted. Let cool on the baking sheet. Transfer to a mason jar and store at room temperature for up to 1 month.

3. To make the Miso Dressing, combine the water, miso, apple cider vinegar, mustard and garlic in a small blender. Whirl until garlic is puréed. Add canola oil and whirl again to combine.

4. To assemble the salad, divide the spinach, radicchio, chickpeas, cucumber and avocado among 4 large bowls or plates. Drizzle each salad with Miso Dressing. Toss well, then sprinkle each salad with about 1 tablespoon of Power Seeds.

Tip Miso is a delicious salty-savoury paste made from fermented soy and grains. It can be white, brown or red—the darker the paste, the stronger the flavour. I use white miso in this dressing, but any type will work. Look for it in the deli or sushi fridge in the supermarket.

Make ahead Make the Miso Dressing and store in the fridge for up to 7 days. Store the Power Seeds at room temperature for up to 1 month.

Batch cooking Both the Power Seeds and the Miso Dressing can be doubled.

Supper Salad

Serves 2 • Make ahead • Batch cooking

A day without green salad is, to me, just not right. Every supper of my childhood featured an oversized salad bowl passed around the table after the main course. (Our French heritage places salad after a meal, not before.) It was a relatively plain assembly of lettuce and a few toppings, dressed with a simple vinaigrette. At our family's table, salad was non-negotiable: you had some or there'd be no dessert. Crunchy, healthy and tangy, it was also a good palate cleanser and belly filler. Green salad became an equally important part of my adult meals. It needn't be elaborate, but to be satisfying, a supper salad has to include lots of lettuce and other crunchy things that take time to chew.

....

1. To make the French Vinaigrette, combine the red wine vinegar with mustard, sugar and salt in a 250 mL jar with a lid and shake well until the sugar and salt are dissolved. Add olive oil and shake well until emulsified. (This makes enough for two batches of this salad.)

2. Tear up the lettuce and divide between 2 large bowls. Top with orange, red pepper and avocado. Drizzle each bowl with about 3 tablespoons vinaigrette and toss well. Sprinkle with feta and Power Seeds, if using.

Make ahead Lettuce can be washed and well dried up to 2 days in advance. Keep it in a large plastic bag with some air in it.

Batch cooking Make a double batch of the vinaigrette and keep it in the fridge for up to 2 weeks.

Prep Time 10 minutes
Ready In about 10 minutes

French Vinaigrette

3 tablespoons red wine vinegar

1 tablespoon Dijon mustard

½ teaspoon granulated sugar

½ teaspoon salt

⅓ cup extra-virgin olive oil

Salad

1 small head leaf lettuce, washed and dried

1 seedless orange, peeled and cut into segments

1 sweet red pepper, sliced

1 avocado, pitted and sliced

½ cup crumbled feta cheese

3 tablespoons Power Seeds (see page 44; optional)

Kale Salad with Bulgur and Feta

Serves 4 • Make ahead

Prep Time 15 minutes or less
Ready In about 20 minutes

1 cup medium-grain bulgur

½ teaspoon salt, divided

1 cup boiling water

3 tablespoons red wine vinegar

1 teaspoon Dijon mustard

½ teaspoon granulated sugar or liquid honey

3 tablespoons extra-virgin olive oil

12 large kale leaves

1 cup crumbled feta cheese

½ cup unsweetened dried cranberries

¼ cup toasted almonds, chopped (optional)

Fresh kale salads are ubiquitous now, but that doesn't make them any less delicious or versatile. Kale is part of the mustard family, and needs strong flavours to match its intensity, so I usually turn to salty feta and sweet-tart cranberries for a perfect combination. To make the salad into a satisfying main dish, I add cooked whole grains such as barley, quinoa or, my new favourite, bulgur. Best of all, these hardy ingredients mean the salad lasts well, so tonight's leftovers will be tomorrow's lunch.

....

1. Combine bulgur and ¼ teaspoon of the salt in a medium bowl. Stir in the boiling water, cover the bowl with a plate and let it stand 5 minutes.

2. Whisk the red wine vinegar with mustard, sugar and the remaining ¼ teaspoon salt in a large bowl. Whisk in the olive oil.

3. Cut out and discard (or freeze, see Tip) the kale stems, then stack the leaves and slice them crosswise into thin strips. You should have about 8 cups, packed. Add kale to the vinaigrette and toss thoroughly. Use a fork to fluff up the bulgur, add it to the kale and toss well—it's fine if the bulgur is still warm. Let this mixture stand 5 minutes.

4. Add the feta and cranberries and toss to combine. Top with almonds, if using. Serve immediately.

Tip 1. Bulgur is a nutritious grain derived from wheat berries. It doesn't need to be cooked, just soaked in hot water (like couscous). It comes in various grades, from fine to very coarse. I prefer medium for this salad, although you can use any grade and follow the package instructions.
2. Coarsely chop kale stems, then freeze them in a resealable plastic bag. Add them to Secretly Green Smoothies (page 34).

Make ahead This salad lasts well in the fridge for up to 1 day. The kale will soften as it sits.

Switch it up Use cooked quinoa or brown rice in place of bulgur.

Split Pea, Butternut and Bacon Soup

Serves 6 • Make ahead • Batch cooking

I love the creaminess of puréed butternut squash soup. However, to make this soup a bit more satisfying, I wanted to add protein, but without taking away from the soup's silky texture. Solution: split peas. Like lentils, split peas are a good source of protein, and once they're fully cooked you can easily purée them smooth. I tend to use a package of pre-cut squash for this recipe simply because it cuts down on the prep time significantly.

....

1. Heat a large soup pot over medium-high heat. Add the bacon and cook about 7 minutes or until crisp. Strain out the bacon with a slotted spoon, leaving about 2 tablespoons of the fat behind. Reserve the bacon.

2. Reduce heat to medium, add the onion and cook, stirring occasionally, 5 minutes or until softened. Add carrots and cook another 2 to 3 minutes. Then add the squash and garlic and cook 2 to 3 minutes or until the garlic is fragrant. Add the split peas, salt, curry powder and cayenne (if using) and stir well. Add the water. Bring to a boil, then reduce heat and simmer, partially covered and stirring often, 55 minutes or until the split peas are completely soft.

3. Purée with an immersion blender or in batches in a blender. If the soup is overly thick, add about ½ cup water.

4. Serve garnished with reserved bacon and a twist of pepper.

Make ahead The soup lasts well in the fridge for up to 3 days. Reheat gently on the stove.

Batch cooking If you have a big enough pot, double the recipe. Let cool completely, then freeze in 2-cup portions for up to 1 month.

Switch it up Make it vegan by omitting the bacon and using a little canola oil to sauté the onions instead. Serve soup sprinkled with roasted chickpeas or nutritional yeast.

Prep Time 10 minutes
Ready In a little over 1 hour

6 to 8 slices bacon, chopped

1 large yellow onion, chopped

2 large carrots, finely chopped

1 pound (450 g) butternut squash, peeled and chopped (about 4 cups)

2 cloves garlic, chopped

1 cup yellow split peas

1 teaspoon salt

½ teaspoon curry powder

⅛ teaspoon cayenne (optional)

7 cups water

Fresh black pepper

Creamy Red Lentil Soup with Warm Spices

Serves 4 • Make ahead • Slow cooker • Batch cooking

Prep Time 10 minutes or less
Ready In about 45 minutes

1½ cups red lentils

7 cups water

¼ cup butter

2 teaspoons ground coriander

2 teaspoons chili powder

1 teaspoon salt

1 teaspoon cinnamon

1 teaspoon ground cumin

½ teaspoon garlic powder

¼ teaspoon ground cardamom (or a pinch of allspice)

¼ teaspoon cayenne (optional)

2 tablespoons liquid honey

Croutons, for garnish

Toasted pepitas, for garnish

There's a wonderful bakery and café in Guelph, Ontario, called With the Grain, where I worked part-time for a few years. I made two soups every day from the café's treasured collection of recipe cards, but every now and then during a busy lunch rush, I'd find myself "in the weeds"—restaurant speak for being up the creek without any soup left in the pot. A simple lentil soup recipe always came to my rescue. Years later, in a pinch about what to make for supper one day, I remembered how easy it was and developed my own. There's nothing to soak, chop or sauté; you just simmer dried lentils with water, then stir in some spiced butter at the end. When I'm in the weeds at home—rushing out the door after breakfast with no plan for dinner—I'll chuck lentils and water in the slow cooker and consider supper all but made.

This is a particularly approachable lentil dish for children. Just omit (or reduce) the cayenne and double the honey.

1. Combine lentils and water in a large pot. Bring to a boil. (Don't leave the pot unattended, as lentils have a tendency to be quiet one moment and boil over furiously the next.) Reduce heat, cover and simmer gently stirring occasionally, for 25 minutes or until the lentils dissolve completely and the soup looks relatively smooth.

2. Melt the butter in a small saucepan over medium heat. Stir in the coriander, chili powder, salt, cinnamon, cumin, garlic powder, cardamom and cayenne (if using), and cook 30 seconds or until fragrant. Stir in the honey, then scrape the mixture into the lentils and stir well to combine.

3. Ladle into 4 bowls and garnish with croutons and pepitas.

Make ahead The soup lasts well in the fridge for up to 3 days. Reheat gently on the stove.

Slow cooker Reduce water to 6 cups. Combine with lentils in a slow cooker and cook on low for 8 hours or on high for 3 hours. The lentils should be completely dissolved and smooth after you stir them a few times. Cook the spiced butter on the stove and add to the soup.

Batch cooking Cool the soup to room temperature, then freeze it in resealable plastic bags or freezer containers for up to 3 months.

Lentil and Vegetable Soup

Serves 4 to 6 • Make ahead • Batch cooking

This is a recipe I make when it seems there isn't much in the pantry. The veggies here last for at least a month in the fridge, and I always have lentils and canned tomatoes in the cupboard. It's also so hearty, but without a morsel of meat. There's not much to the technique, but I like to take the time and care to chop the vegetables in small, evenly sized pieces so every spoonful of soup contains a taste of each one. Lentils are a wonder food: not only are they inexpensive, healthy, delicious and immensely satisfying, they also last indefinitely. Buy a bag today and they'll still be in perfect condition in a year.

1. Heat the canola oil in a large pot over medium-low heat. Add the onion and ¼ teaspoon of the salt. Cover and cook gently, stirring occasionally, 6 to 8 minutes or until the onions are very soft and just starting to brown. Add the carrots and celery and cook, covered, another 3 minutes. Add garlic, cumin and thyme and cook, covered, 1 more minute.

2. Add the tomatoes with their juice, water and Parmesan rind, if using. Increase heat to high and bring to a boil. Add the lentils and remaining ½ teaspoon salt and return to a boil. Reduce heat and simmer, partially covered, 45 minutes or until the lentils are tender.

3. Serve garnished with a sprinkling of parsley and Parmesan and a drizzle of olive oil.

Tip Never throw out the thick rind of a piece of Parmesan. It's chock full of flavour and adds a wonderful richness to vegetarian soups. Rinds will keep well in the freezer for up to 6 months.

Make ahead The soup lasts well in the fridge for up to 5 days. The lentils continue to absorb the liquid, so add a bit of water when reheating.

Batch cooking Double the recipe. Let cool completely, then portion into 2-cup containers or resealable plastic bags. Freeze for up to 1 month.

Prep Time 20 minutes
Ready In a little less than 1 hour

2 tablespoons canola oil

1 medium yellow onion, finely chopped

¾ teaspoon salt, divided

1 large carrot, finely chopped

2 stalks celery, finely chopped

2 cloves garlic, minced

½ teaspoon ground cumin

½ teaspoon dried thyme

1 can (28 ounces/796 mL) whole tomatoes, crushed up by hand

4 cups water

Small Parmesan cheese rind (see Tip; optional)

¾ cup green lentils

For garnish

Chopped fresh parsley

Freshly grated Parmesan cheese

Extra-virgin olive oil

Beef and Barley Soup

Serves 6 • Make ahead • Batch cooking

Prep Time 20 minutes
Ready In about 1 hour

1 tablespoon canola oil

1 boneless beef simmering
steak, such as blade or
cross-rib (12 ounces/340 g)

1½ teaspoons salt, divided

1 medium yellow onion,
chopped

2 carrots, chopped

2 cups peeled and diced
white turnip (about 3 small
turnips)

3 cloves garlic, chopped

1 teaspoon dried thyme

½ cup pearl barley

7 cups water

2 tablespoons tomato paste

1 tablespoon Worcestershire
sauce

People used to say that searing meat before braising is important because it "seals in its juices." That myth has long since been busted, but searing still remains a critical step in building rich, deep flavours in meat dishes. It can feel like an annoying additional step, but it's entirely worth the effort. Searing creates a lovely caramelized flavour not only on the meat but also in the bottom of the pan where the rest of the recipe will be cooked. Without searing, a dish like this tastes a little dull.

This is a simplified way of searing that really reduces the fuss: sear just one slab of meat, then chop it into bite-sized pieces (instead of cutting it up before searing). I never used to make beef-barley soup—even though I love it—because it felt like too much work, but using this technique, it's faster and easier. Thank goodness, because everyone in my extended family adores this soup. It's the perfect cold-weather comfort food.

1. Heat a large soup pot over medium-high heat. Add the canola oil. Sprinkle about ¼ teaspoon of the salt all over the beef. Carefully place the beef in the hot oil and cook about 2 minutes per side or until nicely browned. Transfer beef to a plate. There should be a little oil left in the pot.

2. Reduce heat to medium. Add the onion and cook, stirring occasionally, 3 to 4 minutes or until browned at the edges. Stir in the carrots, turnips and the remaining 1¼ teaspoons salt and cook, stirring occasionally, 3 to 4 minutes or until softened. Add garlic and thyme and cook another 30 seconds. Stir in the barley.

3. Slice the beef into bite-sized strips. Return the beef to the pot along with any accumulated juices on the plate, then add the water and tomato paste. Bring to a boil, then reduce heat, cover and simmer very gently 30 minutes or until the barley is tender. Stir in Worcestershire sauce.

Make ahead Cool the soup to room temperature, then refrigerate for up to 3 days or freeze for up to 1 month. It may need a little extra water once thawed, as the barley will continue to soak up liquid.

Batch cooking Double the recipe. Let cool completely, then freeze in 2-cup portions for up to 1 month.

Switch it up Use the same quantity of parsnips or celery in place of turnips.

Tofu Noodle Soup with Spinach and Cinnamon

Serves 4 • Make ahead

I know tofu is a hard sell for some people, but I swear, between this recipe and Soy-Ginger Tofu (page 139), I can convert anyone to Team Tofu. This recipe is inspired by a Chinese technique of braising beef or pork in a mixture of soy sauce, broth and cinnamon. It sounds a little odd, but the result is extraordinary. Tofu takes well to the same treatment, and quickly soaks up the intense flavours of this broth. This soup is so hearty and warming that I find myself craving it on cold winter nights.

The key to falling in love with tofu is buying the right texture. I don't recommend extra-firm for this recipe. Instead, use firm or medium-firm tofu. The softer texture allows the tofu to better absorb flavour.

....

1. Heat a large pot over medium-high heat. Add the canola and sesame oils, then add the green onions. Cook, stirring often, about 2 minutes or until slightly softened. Add garlic and ginger and cook, stirring, another minute or until fragrant. Add the water and soy sauce and bring to a boil.

2. Add tofu and the cinnamon stick and return to a boil, then reduce heat, cover and simmer gently 15 minutes.

3. Break spaghettini in half and stir into the pot. Cover and simmer 7 to 10 minutes or until noodles are just tender.

4. Turn off heat and stir in spinach and hot sauce.

Tip Tofu comes in various-sized packages. Don't worry too much about buying exactly 1 pound. If you have a little more or a little less, the recipe will still be fine.

Make ahead Make the soup—without the pasta and spinach—up to 2 days ahead. Reheat the soup and then add these two remaining ingredients.

Switch it up Add 1 cup thinly sliced mushrooms along with the spaghettini and ½ cup corn kernels or shelled edamame along with the spinach.

Prep Time 15 minutes
Ready In a little over ½ hour

1 tablespoon canola oil

1 teaspoon sesame oil

4 green onions, chopped

3 cloves garlic, chopped

2 teaspoons chopped fresh ginger

8 cups water

½ cup soy sauce

1 pound (450 g) firm tofu, cut into cubes (see Tip)

1 cinnamon stick, broken in half

3 ounces (85 g) spaghettini

4 cups packed baby spinach

1 teaspoon hot sauce

Chicken

Superfood Chicken Caesar Salad

Serves 2 to 3 • Make ahead

Prep Time 15 minutes
Ready In 15 minutes

1 clove garlic

2 tablespoons fresh
lemon juice

1 tablespoon Dijon mustard

2 teaspoons drained capers

1 anchovy fillet

½ teaspoon Worcestershire
sauce

¼ teaspoon salt

2 tablespoons mayonnaise

¼ cup canola oil

1 package (5 ounces/142 g)
baby kale mix (about 6 cups)

2 cups shredded cooked
chicken

⅓ cup toasted walnut halves,
coarsely chopped

Caesar dressing made this way—like a vinaigrette, not a creamy dressing—is one of my favourite tastes. It's so zingy and flavourful that just thinking about it makes my mouth water. It's versatile too, and I use it not just in this main-dish salad but in all kinds of side salads.

Unlike traditional Caesar dressing, this one has no egg yolk, since I find the combination of Dijon mustard and mayonnaise emulsifies the dressing just as well as an egg yolk would. Tons of Parmesan and croutons usually make Caesar salad less than healthy, so I skip them both in this version and instead add all kinds of nutrient-packed superfoods: anchovy, garlic, canola oil, kale and walnuts. This is a great way to spruce up grocery-store rotisserie chicken.

....

1. Combine the garlic with the lemon juice, mustard, capers, anchovy, Worcestershire sauce and salt in a small blender. Whirl until puréed. Add mayonnaise and whirl to combine. Add canola oil and whirl until emulsified.

2. Combine kale mix with chicken and dressing in a large bowl. Toss well. Divide among bowls and top with walnuts.

Tip Buy anchovies packed in small glass jars instead of the ones in flat tins. It's easier to store a jar than an opened tin, and it's easier to pull out one anchovy at a time.

Make ahead The dressing can be made up to 1 day in advance and stored in the fridge. Shake or whisk well before using.

Switch it up Use chopped romaine lettuce in place of kale mix. Or skip the chicken and walnuts and serve alongside Pan-Seared Rib-Eye Steak (page 88).

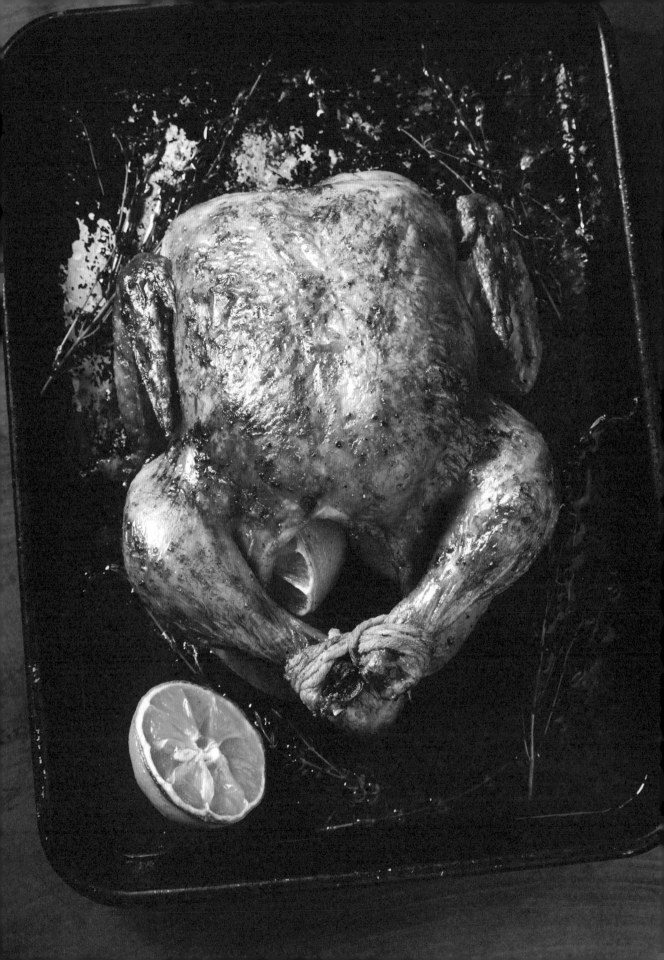

Weekday Roast Chicken

Serves 4

Few dishes say "I'm an accomplished cook" more than a roast chicken. It's also one of those deceptively simple-sounding dishes that actually needs some reverse engineering in order to get it just right. I struggled with roast chicken for years, until I met my partner, Michael, who has been perfecting the art of roast chicken his entire life. His method, in which the bird isn't fully-trussed or stuffed, captures everything I love about uncomplicated cooking: it's fast, smart, easy and delicious. Between this chicken and Michael's duck-fat-roasted potatoes, I was head over heels.

For a weeknight family meal, we have this with a baguette and a big salad or Cabbage with Vinaigrette (page 183) or Minty Peas (page 178). I then use whatever chicken is left over in Easier Chicken and Parmesan Risotto (page 71), Fried Rice with Chicken and Vegetables (page 82) or Grilled Barbecue Chicken Pizza (page 85).

Prep Time 10 minutes or less
Ready In a little over 1 hour

1 best-quality whole chicken (about 3¼ pounds/1.5 kg)

2 tablespoons canola oil

½ teaspoon salt

Handful fresh parsley or thyme sprigs (optional)

½ lemon (optional)

....

1. Preheat the oven to 400°F. Place the chicken breast side up on a rack on a rimmed baking sheet. (The rack isn't necessary, but it helps the chicken cook more evenly; if you don't have one that fits, just place the chicken directly on the baking sheet.) If the chicken came trussed, cut off and remove the twine.

2. Pour the canola oil over the chicken and use your hands or a brush to spread it evenly all over the breast, legs and wings. Sprinkle the whole bird with salt, paying particular attention to the wings. (You can also season all over with fresh black pepper, if you like.) Stuff the parsley and lemon (if using) into the cavity. Tie the legs together with twine if you like.

3. Roast 15 minutes. Reduce heat to 375°F and roast another 45 to 55 minutes or until the chicken is cooked and the skin is deeply golden and slightly crisp. If you poke a sharp knife into the meatiest bit of the thigh, the juices that run out should be clear and not pink. The temperature of the bird (taken in the fleshiest part of the thigh, without touching the bone) should be 175°F.

4. Remove the bird from the oven and let it rest 15 minutes before carving. Serve drizzled with the juices from the baking sheet.

(Recipe continues)

Tip 1. If you start carving the chicken and you realize that it's not quite cooked, don't worry. Cut off the legs and then cut the chicken in half through the breast bone. Place the pieces skin side up in a large frying pan and add all the juices from the baking sheet. Cook over medium-high heat 3 to 7 minutes or until cooked through. **2.** Save the bones in a resealable plastic bag in the freezer for up to 2 months. Use them for Slow-Cooker Chicken Stock (page 67).

Secrets to Success

1. Buy a good chicken. It's easy to make a good chicken taste great (see page 7 for more information).

2. If time allows, put the chicken in a shallow pan and let it sit uncovered in the fridge for up to 24 hours. This lets the outside of the chicken dry, which leads to golden, crispy skin. (No time? Dry the chicken with paper towels like your life depends on it. Don't forget the back and the cavity.)

3. After cooking, let the chicken rest for at least 15 minutes and as much as an hour before carving. Even if you don't follow any of the other secrets to success, follow this one—it's a game changer!

Slow-Cooker Chicken Stock

Makes about 10 cups • Make ahead

In the fine-dining restaurant where I worked in my twenties, we had a pot so big that our pastry chef could actually get into it (which she did for a laugh every now and then). Once a week, we'd fill that pot with chicken bones and vegetable scraps, and two of us would heave the pot up onto the stove at the end of the Sunday evening shift. Once it came to a simmer, we'd turn the flame down to low and go home. Two days later, when we came in at noon to start the work week, the kitchen was filled with the most wonderful smell of chicken stock. Although I worried about leaving the stove on for two days, no one else ever did—that's the way restaurants have been slow-cooking stock for generations.

Now as a homeowner, I'm just as reluctant to leave my gas stove on even for one night, let alone two whole days, so I hacked the old method for the slow cooker. Leaving the lid off might seem wrong, but it's the best way to concentrate the stock. I usually use a mix of fresh chicken backs and necks (inexpensive trim pieces you can get at the butcher) and the frozen carcasses of roast chickens (page 7). Use the stock for Easier Chicken and Parmesan Risotto (page 71) or in place of water for Split Pea, Butternut and Bacon Soup (page 51) or Beef and Barley Soup (page 56).

Prep Time 5 to 10 minutes
Ready In about 36 hours

1½ pounds (675 g) chicken bones, raw or cooked

1 large carrot, not peeled, roughly chopped

2 stalks celery, roughly chopped

1 large yellow onion, not peeled, cut into wedges

3 to 6 small cloves garlic, not peeled

Handful fresh parsley stems or thyme sprigs (optional)

....

1. Place all the chicken bones in the slow cooker. If you have whole carcasses you'll need to break them down (with a knife, or just use your hands and some elbow grease) so that once they're in the slow cooker they sit in an even layer. Add the carrots, celery, onion, garlic and parsley (if using) and stir so they get evenly mixed in with the bones.

2. Pour in enough water to cover the bones by about 1 inch. Cover and cook on high for 5 hours or on low for 12 to 24 hours.

3. Remove the lid, give it a stir, and cook, uncovered, on low for another 6 to 10 hours.

4. Strain the stock and discard the bones, vegetables and parsley. Let cool to room temperature, then chill in the fridge overnight. The fat will congeal on top.

5. Remove and discard the fat layer, then package the stock either in 1 L mason jars or resealable plastic bags.

(Recipe continues)

Tip 1. There is no salt in this recipe because the stock is never eaten as is—it's always incorporated into another recipe. It can be used any time a recipe calls for chicken stock or broth, and it improves the flavour of soups, gravies, risottos and stews. Since it's not salted, taste the recipe often and add salt a little at a time. **2.** This method also works for making turkey stock after you've enjoyed Dry-Brined Turkey (page 213).

Make ahead Store stock in the fridge for up to 1 month or in the freezer for up to 1 year.

Easier Chicken and Parmesan Risotto

Serves 3 to 4

Typically, risotto is made by gradually adding hot stock to rice and stirring, stirring, stirring until the liquid is partially absorbed and partially evaporated. In this easier version, I add the stock in just two batches (instead of the usual ten or twelve) and let time and low heat do the work of stirring. Purists will argue that the result isn't authentic, but it's still creamy and delicious, and it takes half the time and energy to make. I like to serve it with Lemony Broiled Asparagus (page 182), Roasted Broccoli with Lemon and Parmesan (page 188) or Celery and Fennel Salad (page 178). Or, you can leave out the chicken and serve this as a luscious side dish to Weekday Roast Chicken (page 65) or Rosemary-Roasted Pork Tenderloin (page 103).

Prep Time 10 minutes
Ready In about 35 minutes

2 tablespoons butter

1 small yellow onion, very finely chopped

1 cup Arborio rice

¼ cup dry white wine or dry vermouth

3¼ cups Slow-Cooker Chicken Stock (page 67), divided

1½ cups shredded cooked chicken

½ teaspoon salt

½ cup freshly grated Parmesan cheese

Fresh black pepper

Chopped fresh parsley, for garnish

• •

1. Melt the butter in a wide, shallow pan or pot over medium-low heat. Add the onion and cook 5 to 7 minutes or until softened but not browning.

2. Add the rice and stir until well coated with butter. Stir in the white wine and cook until the pan is almost dry.

3. Add 1¾ cups of the chicken stock. Stir well, then leave it alone. After about 5 minutes the pan should be simmering gently. If not, increase the heat a little. Simmer, stirring occasionally, another 5 to 8 minutes or until the liquid has been absorbed, the pan is dry and the risotto is starting to stick to the bottom of the pan. (If pan isn't dry, increase the heat a little until it is.)

4. Scrape the bottom of the pan well, then stir in 1 cup of the chicken stock. Cook, stirring occasionally, another 8 to 10 minutes or until the liquid is absorbed and the rice is tender. If the pan starts to get dry before the rice is tender, add ¼ to ½ cup of the remaining stock. Stir in the chicken and salt and cook 1 minute or until the chicken is heated through.

5. Remove from the heat, stir in the Parmesan and let stand 5 minutes. Serve garnished with pepper and parsley.

Tip 1. It's easy and more than okay to use store-bought chicken broth in place of homemade chicken stock. Choose one that is reduced-sodium and—this is important!—reduce the salt in this recipe, then taste the cooked risotto and add salt as needed for flavour. **2.** It sounds wrong, but for risotto it's a good thing when the rice sticks to the pan. As you scrape it up, rice grains break open and release even more starch into the dish, which adds to the creaminess. Just be sure to really scrape them off the pan so they don't burn.

Spicy Peanut and Lime Noodles with Chicken

Serves 4 • Make ahead

Prep Time 10 minutes
Ready In about 20 minutes

Spicy Peanut Sauce

½ cup natural peanut butter

¼ cup very hot water

¼ cup fresh lime juice

2 tablespoons soy sauce

2 teaspoons liquid honey

1 to 2 teaspoons hot sauce

1 teaspoon finely grated fresh ginger

⅛ teaspoon garlic powder

Lime Noodles and Chicken

8 ounces (225 g) spaghettini

1 cup frozen shelled edamame

2 cups shredded cooked chicken

1 cup thinly sliced red cabbage

For garnish

¼ cup salted roasted peanuts

2 green onions, thinly sliced

Lime wedges

This peanut sauce is so delicious and adds flavour and kick to leftover chicken. It's also a great way to use up those dry last bits of peanut butter from the bottom of the jar. And it's versatile, too: try it on cooked broccoli or carrots, baked tofu, grilled chicken breasts or even a green salad. I love to have cold noodle salads like this one on hot summer evenings, and the zing of spice and lime here is particularly refreshing. I use regular pasta, but substitute whatever noodles you like.

1. To make the Spicy Peanut Sauce, combine the peanut butter, hot water, lime juice, soy sauce, honey, hot sauce, ginger and garlic powder in a small blender and purée until smooth. Alternatively, you can whisk it like crazy until emulsified. If it's too thick, add 1 to 2 tablespoons hot water.

2. Boil spaghettini in a large pot of salted water until just tender, about 7 minutes or according to package directions. One minute before it's done, stir in the edamame. Drain the whole pot and rinse both the pasta and the edamame with lots of cold running water.

3. Combine cooled pasta and edamame with chicken, cabbage and three-quarters of the Spicy Peanut Sauce. Toss very well, adding the remaining peanut sauce if you like the dish saucier (or save sauce for another use).

4. Divide among 4 bowls and top with peanuts and green onions. Serve with lime wedges.

Tip Frozen edamame are a boon to weekday cooking, and kids love them. Make sure to get the already shelled ones to make your life easier.

Make ahead The Spicy Peanut Sauce lasts well in the fridge for up to 5 days.

Teriyaki Chicken Skewers

Serves 4 • Make ahead

Rare is the person who can turn down teriyaki chicken. There's nothing fancy about it, but the combination of soy sauce, brown sugar, ginger and a hot grill is kind of extraordinary. I love that the marinating time can be short or long, and that all these ingredients are sitting in the fridge and pantry right now just waiting to be put to work. Because fresh ginger tends to burn on the grill, I use the powder instead. Serve with basmati rice, Grilled Corn (page 185) or a pile of green beans. Or use it as the chicken component of Spicy Peanut and Lime Noodles with Chicken (page 72).

••

1. Whisk the soy sauce with sugar, rice vinegar, chili-garlic sauce (if using), ginger and garlic in a shallow dish (such as a glass pie plate) that can accommodate all the chicken in a single layer.

2. Cut the chicken into 2-inch cubes. Add to the marinade and stir well to coat. Marinate at room temperature for 20 minutes.

3. Meanwhile, soak 4 bamboo skewers in warm water for 15 minutes. Preheat the grill to high.

4. Thread chicken pieces onto each skewer, snuggling them up against each other fairly tightly. Reserve the marinade.

5. Grease the grill very well, then add the skewers. Grill, with the lid closed, 2 minutes. Brush chicken with some of the reserved marinade, then flip, close the lid and grill another 2 minutes. Baste one more time, then reduce heat to medium-low, close the lid and grill another 12 to 16 minutes or until cooked through and springy to the touch. Take skewers off the grill and drizzle with honey, if using. Serve immediately.

Tip Rice vinegar is often sold "seasoned," which means it has added sugar and salt. Tasty, but unnecessary in this application. But if seasoned rice vinegar is all you have, feel free to use it.

Make ahead Marinate the chicken in the fridge for up to 1 day.

Prep Time 15 minutes
Ready In about 1 hour

3 tablespoons soy sauce

2 tablespoons brown sugar

1 teaspoon rice vinegar

1 teaspoon hot chili-garlic sauce (optional)

¼ teaspoon ground ginger

2 large cloves garlic, peeled and cut in half

1½ pounds (675 g) boneless, skinless chicken (about 3 breasts or 6 thighs)

1 tablespoon liquid honey (optional)

Coconut Chicken Curry

Serves 4 to 6 • Make ahead

Prep Time 20 minutes
Ready In about 50 minutes

2 tablespoons canola oil

1 medium yellow onion, finely chopped

½ teaspoon salt

3 cloves garlic, chopped

2 teaspoons grated fresh ginger

3 tablespoons Indian curry paste

¼ teaspoon cayenne (optional)

⅛ teaspoon cinnamon

1½ pounds (675 g) boneless, skinless chicken, cut into 2-inch cubes (about 6 thighs or 3 breasts)

1 can (14 ounces/398 mL) chopped tomatoes (see page 4)

1 can (14 ounces/400 mL) full-fat coconut milk

1½ cups frozen peas

Chopped fresh cilantro, for garnish

I find it really hard to name my favourite foods (because I have so many, and the list is always changing), but curry is always included in the rundown. I particularly love the simplicity of this one, which is seasoned with good-quality curry paste (the kind you keep in the fridge) and cinnamon. That spice combination, along with chicken, tomato and coconut, is sweet and interesting, and appealing to all ages and stages, whether this is someone's first curry or their hundredth.

This is a saucy curry, and in my house we eat it plain like a chunky soup. To make it a little bit thicker, use only half a can of coconut milk (or a 5.5-ounce/160 mL can). Freeze the rest of the coconut milk for up to 6 months. Serve the curry with rice to soak up the sauce if you like.

1. Heat the canola oil in a large non-stick frying pan over medium-high heat. Add the onion and salt and cook, stirring occasionally, 5 minutes or until the onion softens and just starts to get golden. Stir in the garlic and ginger and cook 1 minute.

2. Stir in the curry paste, cayenne (if using) and cinnamon, then add chicken and stir to coat. Cook 3 minutes, stirring occasionally, then stir in the tomatoes. Reduce heat to low, cover and cook 5 minutes.

3. Stir in the coconut milk. When the curry starts to simmer again, stir in peas and cook another 3 to 5 minutes or until everything is hot. Serve garnished with cilantro.

Tip I much prefer full-fat coconut milk over light. It brings so much more flavour and a luscious texture to the dish. Sometimes the fat will separate away from the liquid in the can—don't worry, just add the can's contents to the curry and stir it in (or give the can a good shake before you open it).

Make ahead This curry keeps well in the fridge for up to 2 days.

Lemon and Spice Grilled Chicken

Serves 4 • Make ahead

In cooking, it often seems the simplest things are often the trickiest to get right. I'm not sure why that is, but I get more questions about grilling chicken pieces than about almost anything else. It should be effortless to get juicy yet crisp and golden pieces off the grill, right? Nope. But after struggling with grilled chicken myself, I finally cracked the code. Putting the pieces on when the grill is very hot and just freshly greased—and not touching them for several minutes—is the key to avoiding having the chicken stick, and cooking chicken slow and low keeps it juicy on the inside while letting it cook through. Serve with Grilled Corn (page 185) and Carrot-Lemon Slaw (page 189).

....

1. Combine the lemon juice with the coriander, thyme, salt, garlic powder, onion powder and paprika (if using) in a resealable plastic bag. Add the chicken pieces, close up the bag and wriggle it a bit to get the chicken nicely coated. Let stand on the counter for 20 minutes.

2. Preheat the grill to high. Once it's hot, spray the grill generously with non-stick cooking spray. Place chicken pieces skin side down on the hot grill. Cook, with the lid closed, 3 minutes. Turn the pieces and reduce heat to medium-low. Cook, with the lid closed, 17 to 20 minutes or until cooked through and very springy when pressed.

Tip Garlic and onion powders (not salts) are dehydrated versions of the real thing and are extremely useful in grilling and slow-cooking recipes, where the fresh versions can burn or turn acrid. Also, they last over a year and require no chopping.

Make ahead Prepare the marinated chicken (step 1, above) and store in the fridge up to 24 hours before cooking.

Prep Time 5 minutes
Ready In less than 1 hour

½ cup fresh lemon juice
(about 2 lemons)

2 teaspoons ground coriander

1 teaspoon dried thyme

½ teaspoon salt

½ teaspoon garlic powder

¼ teaspoon onion powder

¼ teaspoon smoked paprika
(optional)

2 bone-in, skin-on chicken breasts

2 bone-in, skin-on chicken legs

Secret-Ingredient Chicken Burgers with Cilantro Salsa

Serves 4 • Make ahead • Batch cooking

Prep Time 10 minutes
Ready In less than 20 minutes

1 pound (450 g) ground chicken

1 green onion, finely chopped

1 clove garlic, grated

½ cup panko crumbs

2 tablespoons fish sauce

1 teaspoon hot chili-garlic sauce (optional)

Canola oil

Cilantro Salsa

1 cup chopped fresh cilantro

1 green onion, finely chopped

1 small hot chili pepper, finely chopped (optional)

2 tablespoons fresh lime juice

⅛ teaspoon salt

For Serving

4 burger buns

Boston or leaf lettuce

Sliced tomatoes

Until I discovered these, my reaction to chicken burgers was always a shrug and a "meh." They're usually just so bland. But here the salty, umami richness of fish sauce ignites plain old chicken burgers and makes them exceptionally tasty. Fish sauce is common in Southeast Asian cuisines, and although it may sound intimidating, it is anything but. Used in small amounts, it's the secret miracle ingredient that takes recipes from good to unforgettable, and you never taste fish—just rich flavour. These burgers are a bit too lean and delicate for the barbecue, so cook them on the stove instead. Serve with Sweet-and-Sour Bok Choy (page 179) or Celery and Fennel Salad (page 178).

1. Mix the chicken, green onion, garlic, panko, fish sauce and chili-garlic sauce (if using) in a large bowl until well combined. Shape the mixture into 4 patties, each about ½ inch thick.

2. To make the Cilantro Salsa, stir the cilantro with green onion, chili pepper (if using), lime juice and salt.

3. Heat a large non-stick frying pan over medium heat. Brush the patties with a bit of canola oil, then cook 2 to 3 minutes per side or until golden. Reduce heat to low and cook 4 to 7 minutes or until cooked through.

4. Serve burgers on buns with lettuce, tomato and Cilantro Salsa.

Make ahead Mix the chicken and seasonings, shape into patties and keep refrigerated for up to 12 hours.

Batch cooking The recipe doubles—or even triples—well. Shape into patties and freeze in a single layer or with parchment paper dividers between each patty. Seal well and keep frozen for up to 1 month. Thaw fully in the fridge before cooking.

Fried Rice with Chicken and Vegetables

Serves 4

Prep Time 15 minutes
Ready In about ½ hour

2 tablespoons canola oil

5 teaspoons chopped fresh ginger

2 to 3 cloves garlic, thinly sliced

1 yellow onion, thinly sliced

1 cup small-chopped broccoli

⅛ teaspoon salt

1 sweet red or yellow pepper, chopped

3 cups cold day-old white rice

2 eggs

1½ cups shredded cooked chicken

2 to 3 tablespoons soy sauce

1 tablespoon sesame oil

I never gave fried rice the time of day until I discovered world-famous French chef Jean-Georges Vongerichten's version. Chef Vongerichten shallow-fries ginger, garlic, leeks and other ingredients separately before carefully combining everything in one bowl. It is exceptionally delicious . . . and a little too complicated for my everyday life. Since we often have leftover rice, either from a previous supper or a Thai delivery, I simplified Jean-Georges's concept and came up with this shortcut. Now this is a fast weeknight one-pot wonder meal that you can adjust to suit your tastes and what's in the fridge.

1. Heat the canola oil in a large non-stick frying pan over medium-low heat. Add the ginger and garlic and cook, stirring often, 2 minutes or until softened. Add the onion and cook another 2 minutes, increasing the heat if the onion isn't sizzling gently. Add the broccoli and salt and cook another 2 minutes. Add the peppers and cook 1 minute.

2. Stir in the rice and cook, stirring often, 2 to 3 minutes or until rice is very hot.

3. Make a little space in the centre of the pan and crack in the eggs. Using a wooden spoon or silicone spatula, mix up the eggs. They will start to cook, so start incorporating quickly into the rice, stirring constantly until the egg cooks and the pan looks dry.

4. Stir in the chicken and cook until everything is piping hot. Remove from the heat and stir in the soy sauce and sesame oil. Serve immediately.

Tip Day-old rice works best, but if you're desperate for fried rice now, cook the rice, spread it out on a baking sheet and pop it in the fridge to cool completely before using it.

Switch it up You can use almost any vegetable in this dish, from frozen edamame to canned corn to zucchini. The same goes for the protein: use cooked shrimp or beef or tofu.

Grilled Barbecue Chicken Pizza

Serves 3 to 4 • Make ahead

This pizza is pure joy. It might seem like a bad idea for a number of reasons—throwing raw dough directly on the grill sounds unwise, for starters—but it always turns out amazingly well, and it's also a wonderful twist on regular pizza. In most pizzerias, barbecue chicken pizza is made up of tomato sauce and chicken tossed with barbecue sauce, but I prefer to cut out the middleman and just use barbecue sauce where the tomato sauce should be. It's salty, sweet, spicy and crazy good. Serve it with Celery and Fennel Salad (page 178) or Carrot-Lemon Slaw (page 189).

••

1. Preheat the grill to high. Dust a large baking sheet with flour.

2. Roll out the dough on a lightly floured counter, using a lightly floured rolling pin, into a 12-inch circle (it's okay if it looks uneven). Transfer it to the baking sheet to take it out it to the grill.

3. Prep all the other ingredients and bring them out to the grill too. Bring a spoon and a pair of tongs.

4. Grease the grill generously with non-stick cooking spray. Using both hands (and all your courage), stretch out the dough and flop it as evenly as possible onto the hot grill. As soon as it hits the grill, you still have a few seconds to use your tongs to adjust its shape. Close the lid and cook 1 to 1½ minutes. The bottom should be firm and slightly charred.

5. Use tongs to flip the dough over, then immediately reduce heat to low. Working fairly quickly, spread barbecue sauce all over the dough. Sprinkle with half the mozzarella, the chicken, onion, pineapple and hot peppers, if using. Top with the remaining mozzarella. Close the lid and cook 6 to 8 minutes or until the cheese is melted.

6. Lift the pizza back onto the baking sheet to take it to the table. Sprinkle with cilantro, if using.

Make ahead Prep all the toppings up to 12 hours in advance, then just heat the grill, roll the dough and it's pizza time.

Prep Time 15 minutes
Ready In about ½ hour if dough is ready

½ batch pizza dough (see page 132 or 1 pound/ 450g store-bought)

½ cup barbecue sauce

2 cups shredded mozzarella cheese, divided

1 cup shredded cooked chicken

½ small red onion, thinly sliced

½ cup pineapple chunks

½ cup pickled hot pepper rings (optional)

Chopped fresh cilantro (optional)

Beef, Pork and Lamb

Pan-Seared Rib-Eye Steak

Serves 2 to 3

Prep Time 5 minutes or less
Ready In about 25 minutes

1 boneless rib-eye steak,
1½ to 2 inches thick (about
1 pound/450 g)

1 teaspoon kosher salt

1 tablespoon butter, at room
temperature

Steak is just about as good as dinner gets, in my eyes. Whenever we celebrate anything—a birthday, Valentine's Day or just a lovely summer Friday—Michael and I always have steak. For a first-class experience, you'll want a tender, flavourful cut of beef. Rib-eye is my favourite, but strip loin is a decent second choice. Tenderloin isn't tasty enough, and everything else is just a bit too tough in texture to be truly luxurious. (Don't get me wrong, I love all cuts of beef, but we're talking about special dinners here.)

To serve two to three people, you'll want one steak that is almost 2 inches thick. (If you don't see it in the counter display, ask the butcher if he can cut it fresh for you. Most will be happy to do so.) And don't mess with it. Season it generously with kosher salt (one of the few times when regular table salt won't do), sear it in a blisteringly hot pan, then let it cook gently until medium-rare. This is a simple dish, but it packs a flavour wallop. Keep it simple with Jacket Potatoes (page 184) and Caesar Salad (page 62 without the chicken and walnuts).

....

1. Pat the steak dry with paper towels. Sprinkle both sides of the steak evenly and generously with salt. It might look like too much, but remember you'll be serving it sliced.

2. Heat a heavy frying pan over high heat for at least 2 minutes. Place the steak in the dry pan and cook 2 minutes. Flip the steak and cook another 1 minute. Reduce heat to medium-low and cook 8 to 12 minutes or until medium-rare (135°F to 140°F).

3. Put the butter on the steak and wait 10 seconds, then transfer the steak to a platter.

4. Rest the steak, uncovered, at least 5 minutes but up to 15 minutes. Carve into ½-inch-thick slices to serve.

Tip Pan-searing a rib-eye indoors can be noisy. As the fat from the steak renders, it smokes and can sometimes set off the fire alarm. My solution is to cook it in a cast-iron pan on the barbecue. Place the cast-iron pan on the barbecue and preheat to high with the lid closed. Cook the steak as above, keeping the lid closed.

Herb and Garlic Meatloaf

Serves 6 • Make ahead • Batch cooking

When it comes to uncomplicated cooking, meatloaf is a champion. It's classic comfort food, the kind of cozy, familiar dish that everyone loves. Prepping meatloaf takes just minutes, and you can have it on the table in less than an hour. It can be made ahead, doubled to feed a crowd, or frozen and sent along to a new parent or busy student. As well, there may be nothing finer in the world than a leftover meatloaf sandwich. My version is tender thanks to a mixture of pork, beef and breadcrumbs. I use the trick of grating the onions and garlic (instead of chopping them) so they disperse more evenly in the mixture and essentially disappear during cooking. I adore this dish, and often make it early in the week so we can have it for lunches for the next few days. Serve it with mashed potatoes and Curry-Spiced Roasted Squash (page 188).

....

1. Preheat the oven to 325°F.

2. Mix the beef, pork, onion, garlic, eggs, panko, ketchup, parsley, Worcestershire sauce, thyme and salt in a large bowl until well combined. Pack the mixture into a 9- x 5-inch loaf pan and smooth the top.

3. Brush the top with HP sauce. Bake 60 to 70 minutes or until the blade of a paring knife poked into the centre of the loaf is hot to the touch.

Tip Breadcrumbs do a lot of the work in this mixture. They make the texture even and light, and help all the flavours to blend. It doesn't matter if you use panko crumbs, unseasoned Italian breadcrumbs or breadcrumbs you make yourself.

Make ahead Mix the ingredients and keep the mixture in the fridge for up to 12 hours before transferring it to the loaf pan and baking it. You can also cook the meatloaf, take it out of the pan, chill it and reheat it any time in the following 2 days. It's also delicious cold.

Batch cooking Double the recipe and portion it into two loaves. Wrap each one individually in plastic wrap, then freeze in a resealable plastic bag for up to 1 month. Thaw overnight in the fridge, then transfer to a loaf pan to bake.

Prep Time 10 minutes
Ready In less than ½ hour

1 pound (450 g) lean ground beef

1 pound (450 g) ground pork

1 small yellow onion, grated

2 cloves garlic, grated

2 eggs

½ cup panko crumbs or dry breadcrumbs

⅓ cup ketchup

¼ cup finely chopped fresh parsley

1 tablespoon Worcestershire sauce

1 teaspoon dried thyme

1 teaspoon salt

2 tablespoons HP sauce (or extra ketchup)

Gingery Beef and Broccoli with Cashews

Serves 4 • Make ahead

Prep Time 25 minutes
Ready In a little over ½ hour

Marinated Beef

1 flank steak or boneless blade steak (about 1 pound/450 g)

2 tablespoons soy sauce

1 tablespoon cornstarch

1 tablespoon chopped fresh ginger

Stir-Fry Sauce

¼ cup dry white wine

¼ cup water

2 tablespoons soy sauce

1 tablespoon granulated sugar

1 tablespoon cornstarch

1 to 3 teaspoons hot chili-garlic sauce (optional)

Stir-Fry

1 large bunch broccoli, cut into small florets (about 4 cups)

¼ cup water

1 tablespoon canola oil

4 cloves garlic, chopped

1 tablespoon chopped fresh ginger

⅓ cup salted roasted cashews or peanuts

Make ahead All the components can be assembled up to 1 day in advance: marinate the beef (let it marinate the whole time), cut up the broccoli and make the sauce.

Stir-fries are a boon to the time-starved weekday cook. They take some prep work up front, but once you get started cooking, dinner is minutes away. Classically, stir-fries are made in a wok, but I get better, higher heat in my largest non-stick frying pan. For maximum efficiency, start by marinating the beef (and cooking rice if you like), then mix up the sauce and prep the remaining ingredients while the beef sits.

This recipe works well with chicken and different vegetables, but I recommend starting with this unbeatable combination of beef, broccoli, ginger and nuts, which is one of my all-time favourites. Serve with rice or rice noodles if you like.

....

1. To prepare the Marinated Beef, cut the flank steak into 2 pieces, slicing with the grain, then slice it against the grain as thinly as possible. Place the slices in a medium bowl and stir in the soy sauce, cornstarch and ginger. Stir well, then let marinate at room temperature about 20 minutes.

2. To make the Stir-Fry Sauce, stir the white wine, water, soy sauce, sugar, cornstarch and chili-garlic sauce (if using) together in a bowl or measuring cup. Reserve.

3. Combine the broccoli and water in a large non-stick frying pan with a lid. Bring to a boil and cook, covered, 2 to 4 minutes or until the broccoli is just barely tender-crisp and the pan is dry. Transfer broccoli to a bowl or plate.

4. Put the pan back on the stove over medium-high heat. Add the canola oil, then the beef mixture with the marinade. Spread the beef into an even layer and cook 1 minute, then stir while cooking for another 1 to 2 minutes or until the beef is mostly cooked.

5. Add the garlic and ginger and cook, stirring, 1 minute. Return the broccoli to the pan and stir well.

6. Stir the sauce, then add it all at once and stir until it thickens, about 30 seconds. Sprinkle with cashews. Serve immediately.

Tip To slice steak as thinly as possible, pop it into the freezer for 20 to 30 minutes first. Semi-frozen beef is much easier to cut. You can add the slices to the marinade immediately.

Soy and Garlic Grilled Flank Steak

Serves 4 • Make ahead

Flank steak used to be considered a cheap cut of meat—one that needed to marinate for a long time in order to be anything close to edible. It's more popular now (and consequently not quite as inexpensive), but there still exists a misconception that it must be marinated. The truth is, flank steak is always tender as long as you slice it against the grain. That way, you shorten the long fibres of the meat, making it much easier and more pleasant to chew. To me, it's actually a win-win: flank steak is sturdy enough to stand up to a long marination, so you can get it started well in advance of cooking if you have the time, but you can also just give it a quick soak and be digging in half an hour later. This marinade adds a sophisticated sweet-and-sour flavour, delicious hot off the grill or cold on tomorrow's salad. Most often, we enjoy these steaks with Jacket Potatoes (page 184) and Celery and Fennel Salad (page 178).

Prep Time 5 minutes or less
Ready In a little over ½ hour

3 tablespoons red wine vinegar

2 tablespoons ketchup

2 tablespoons soy sauce

½ teaspoon garlic powder

1 flank steak (about 1½ pounds/ 675 g)

Flaky sea salt and fresh black pepper, for serving

1. Mix the red wine vinegar, ketchup, soy sauce and garlic powder together in a resealable plastic bag. Add the steak, close the bag, squeezing out the air, and marinate 20 minutes at room temperature.

2. Preheat the grill to medium-high. Spray the grill well with non-stick cooking spray, then lift the steak out of its marinade and grill, turning once, 3 to 5 minutes per side for medium-rare.

3. Let the steak rest for at least 5 minutes, then slice it thinly across the grain. Serve hot, room temperature or cold, sprinkled with flaky salt and pepper.

Make ahead Marinate the steak in the fridge for up to 24 hours.

Saucy Pot Roast

Serves 6 to 8 • Make ahead

Prep Time 20 minutes
Ready In about 4½ hours

¼ cup all-purpose flour

1 teaspoon dried thyme

½ teaspoon salt, divided

1 beef pot roast, such as cross-rib or blade (about 3 pounds/1.35 kg)

2 tablespoons canola oil

1½ cups dry red wine

3 cups beef broth

1 yellow onion, chopped

2 large carrots, chopped

3 stalks celery, chopped

1 large clove garlic, sliced

Chopped fresh parsley, for garnish

Make ahead Make the pot roast up to 3 days in advance. Store the meat and sauce in the fridge, then heat them together, covered, at 325°F for about 1 hour.

Pot roast has a terrible reputation in popular culture for being grey and tough, with watery sauce. It's such a shame, because pot roast is a wonderful comfort food, and it's the first thing I want to cook when the weather turns chilly. Pot roast is simply beef stew without all the little pieces of meat. It's faster and easier to sear one large piece of meat than many small pieces, and I've simplified it even further by tossing chopped vegetables into the liquid (rather than sautéing them first). Long, slow cooking makes the beef and vegetables tender and flavourful, and the whole concoction smells so good your neighbours may knock on the door and beg for an invitation to dinner. And it is an excellent dish for entertaining, since one pot roast feeds many, all the work is done in advance and it's so delicious.

The sauce longs for something to soak it up—think mashed potatoes, polenta, plain pasta or good bread. Add a green vegetable such as Lemony Broiled Asparagus (page 182) or Roasted Broccoli with Lemon and Parmesan (page 188).

··

1. Preheat the oven to 325°F.

2. Stir the flour with the thyme and ¼ teaspoon of the salt in a shallow dish. Dry the beef with paper towels, then roll it around in the flour mixture, knocking off the excess. It should be just barely coated.

3. Heat a large, deep oven-safe pot or Dutch oven over medium-high heat. Add the canola oil. Add the beef and cook 2 minutes per side or until each side is deeply golden, reducing the heat as needed so the pan doesn't burn. Transfer the beef to a plate. (If the oil has burned a little, just wipe out the pan with paper towel.)

4. Pour the red wine and beef broth into the pot and bring to a boil. Add the onion, carrots, celery, garlic and remaining ¼ teaspoon salt. Once this mixture is simmering, return the beef, along with any accumulated juices, to the pot, shifting the veggies so the beef sits on the bottom of the pot. The liquid should go about halfway up the roast. Cover the pot and put it in the oven for 3 hours.

5. Give it a stir, turn over the meat and cook, partially covered, another 45 minutes or until the sauce thickens a bit.

6. Take the beef out of the sauce and slice it in ½-inch to 1-inch slices. Spoon some sauce and vegetables over the meat. Garnish with parsley. Serve the rest of the sauce alongside.

Italian Meatballs with Lemon and Parsley

Serves 4 • Make ahead • Batch cooking

My dad, Brian, loves to eat, but he only cooks a few things. His portfolio includes scrambled eggs, corned beef hash, cedar-planked salmon and these meatballs. Spending an entire afternoon at the kitchen counter rolling these, and then carefully sautéing them in batches, is one of his favourite ways to spend time with his beloved grandchildren. I respectfully—and lovingly—simplify and speed things up by making them a little bigger and broiling them instead, so we can have them even on a busy weeknight. I usually serve these on toasted buns or toss them with Uncomplicated Tomato Sauce (page 162) and serve them over cooked pasta with salad or Roasted Broccoli with Lemon and Parmesan (page 188) alongside.

....

1. Position one oven rack so it's about 8 inches away from the broiler and preheat the oven to 400°F. Line a rimmed baking sheet with foil and spray it with non-stick cooking spray (you might need 2 baking sheets).

2. Combine the ground beef, sausages, panko, Parmesan, parsley, garlic, lemon zest and salt in a large bowl and mix until well combined. Shape the mixture into balls about 1½ inches in diameter. Place meatballs on the prepared baking sheet about 1½ inches apart.

3. Bake 15 minutes or until cooked through. Switch oven to broil. Broil 2 minutes, watching very carefully, or until the tops are sizzling and dark brown.

Make ahead Roll the meatballs and keep them (on the baking sheet) in the fridge for up to 12 hours.

Batch cooking Roll meatballs and freeze them (uncooked) right on an unlined baking sheet. Once frozen, transfer to a resealable plastic bag and keep frozen for up to 1 month. Thaw overnight in the fridge before cooking. Or, to cook directly from frozen, reduce oven temperature to 350°F and cook 35 minutes before broiling as per the recipe.

Prep Time 25 minutes
Ready In about 45 minutes

1 pound (450 g) lean ground beef

2 mild Italian sausages, casings removed

½ cup panko crumbs

⅓ cup freshly grated Parmesan cheese

2 tablespoons finely chopped parsley

2 cloves garlic, minced

Zest of 1 lemon

¾ teaspoon salt

Naked Burgers

Serves 4 • Make ahead • Batch cooking

Prep Time less than 10 minutes
Ready In about 20 minutes

1½ pounds (675 g) medium ground beef

½ teaspoon salt

Fresh black pepper

Why are these burgers naked? Take a look: this recipe contains no eggs, breadcrumbs, onion soup mix or any of the other usual burger-mix additions. Consider this a burger make-under, because it turns out that burgers don't need any of that extra junk. I once conducted an elaborate blind tasting of different burger mixes. The one everyone liked best was . . . just beef and salt. The joke was on me: that's the way my dad has been making burgers for forty years.

I serve these on toasted whole wheat buns slathered with ketchup, Dijon mustard and mayonnaise, with plates of thinly sliced red onions, cucumbers, hot fresh chilies and pickles alongside so people can top their burgers however they like.

....

1. Line a rimmed baking sheet with parchment paper. Shape the meat into 4 equal patties on the baking sheet, using a 3½-inch round cookie cutter to shape the burgers so they are evenly sized and flat all the way across. Sprinkle each one with salt on each side. Season with pepper.

2. Heat a frying pan (not non-stick; I use cast iron) over high heat. When it's hot, place the patties in the dry pan and cook 2 minutes. Flip the burgers and cook another 2 minutes. Reduce heat to low and cook 2 to 5 more minutes or until just cooked through. Serve on buns with your favourite toppings.

Tip 1. Medium ground beef has a higher fat content than lean (obviously), which means it splatters more as it cooks, but the burgers end up tastier and much more tender. **2.** If you want to take your cooking outside, cook on high heat on a well-greased grill for about the same amount of time.

Make ahead Shape the patties, cover loosely with plastic wrap and keep them in the fridge for up to 12 hours. Season with salt and pepper just before cooking.

Batch cooking Shape the patties but do not season them. Freeze them, separated by little squares of parchment paper, in a resealable plastic bag, for up to 6 weeks. Thaw in the fridge overnight. Season with salt and pepper just before cooking.

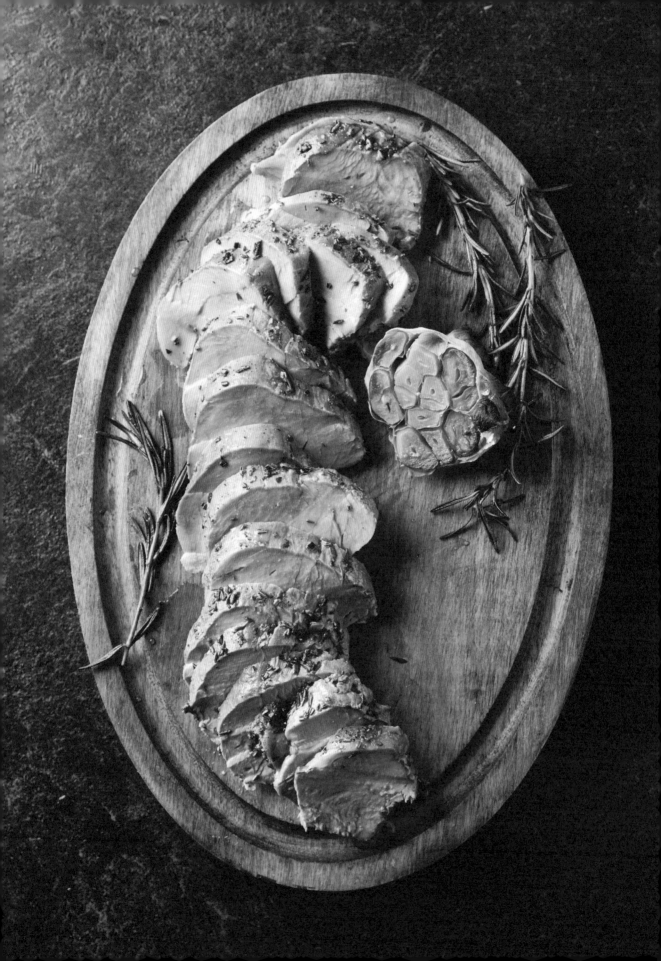

Rosemary-Roasted Pork Tenderloin

Serves 2

Pork tenderloin is easy to cook and even easier to serve. It's fairly mild, but fresh rosemary and Dijon mustard bring out its best. We eat it often during the week, since it's a fast roast, and because it's an easygoing dinner that my son has enjoyed since his toddler days, although these days we usually have to double the recipe to accommodate his growing appetite! The size of tenderloins varies widely from store to store—I often find them closer to 1½ pounds (675 g). If that's what you have, just add more rosemary and 5 to 10 minutes to the cooking time. This goes well with many dishes, although Curry-Spiced Roasted Squash (page 188) and Carrot-Lemon Slaw (page 189) are both particularly good matches.

Prep Time 10 minutes or less
Ready In a little over ½ hour

1 pound (450 g) pork tenderloin

¼ teaspoon salt

1 tablespoon Dijon mustard

1 tablespoon chopped fresh rosemary

Fresh black pepper

....

1. Preheat the oven to 450°F. Line a small roasting pan with parchment paper.

2. Dry the pork with paper towel, then sprinkle all over with salt. Place pork in the prepared pan, then smear with mustard. Sprinkle evenly with rosemary. Season with pepper.

3. Roast 10 minutes. Reduce heat to 350°F and roast another 16 to 22 minutes or until a thermometer inserted into the centre reads 160°F. Let rest for 5 minutes, then slice.

One-Pan Roast Sausage Supper

Serves 3 to 4

Prep Time 20 minutes
Ready In about 1 hour

1 sweet red pepper, thinly sliced

1 small acorn squash, scrubbed, seeded and cut into ¼-inch wedges

1 yellow onion, thinly sliced

6 sprigs fresh thyme

3 tablespoons canola oil, divided

4 to 6 Italian sausages

¼ teaspoon salt, divided

Fresh black pepper

6 kale leaves, roughly torn

Whenever I make this dish, I wonder why we don't have it more often. It's so easy and delicious—and clean-up is such a snap—that it really is a perfect weeknight meal. As soon as you walk into the kitchen, turn on the oven. By the time it's preheated, your pan of ingredients will be ready to cook, leaving you a little over half an hour to unload the dishwasher, make tomorrow's lunch or just stare off into space with a glass of wine. Serve this as is or with good bread.

....

1. Preheat the oven to 400°F. Line a large rimmed baking sheet or shallow roasting pan with parchment paper.

2. Put the red pepper, squash, onion and thyme sprigs on the pan and drizzle with 2 tablespoons of the canola oil. Toss well and spread out in a single layer. Nestle the sausages in between the vegetables. Sprinkle with ⅛ teaspoon of the salt and season with pepper. Roast 25 to 30 minutes.

3. Toss the kale with the remaining 1 tablespoon canola oil and remaining ⅛ teaspoon salt. Turn the sausages, then sprinkle torn kale evenly over the pan. Roast another 7 minutes or until the kale wilts and the other vegetables are tender and golden. Serve immediately.

Slow-Cooker Sweet and Spicy Ribs

Serves 4 • Make ahead

Prep Time less than
10 minutes
Ready In about 4 hours

2 racks pork back ribs (about
2 pounds/900 g total)

¼ to 1 teaspoon cayenne

½ teaspoon garlic powder

½ teaspoon onion powder

½ teaspoon smoked paprika

½ teaspoon salt

½ cup packed brown sugar

¼ cup soy sauce

¼ cup water

1 tablespoon apple cider
vinegar

For many years, I didn't understand the appeal of ribs. The meat is often dry and stringy, and there's so little of it left on the bones that you're really just eating sweet barbecue sauce. Then I tasted slow-cooker ribs and I got it. These are tender and infused with tons of flavour. They aren't authentic at all—in fact they're barely in the same ballpark as true Southern barbecue ribs—but they make an easy, tasty weeknight supper. This dry rub is also delicious on pork tenderloin or chops. Boiled potatoes, Lemony Broiled Asparagus (page 182) and Grilled Corn (page 185) round the ribs out nicely.

....

1. Cut each rack of ribs into 2 or 3 pieces. Stir the spices and salt together in a small bowl. Rub the mix all over the ribs, then place ribs in the slow cooker.

2. Stir the brown sugar with soy sauce, water and apple cider vinegar in a small bowl. Once the brown sugar is mostly dissolved, pour this mixture into the slow cooker.

3. Cover and cook on high for 4 hours or on low for 8 to 10 hours. The ribs are fine to eat now, but a little unsightly. Take the ribs out of the slow cooker and place them on a rimmed baking sheet lined with foil.

4. Preheat the broiler. Strain the sauce from the slow cooker, skim off and discard most of the fat, then put the sauce in a wide frying pan. Boil the sauce over high heat until thickened, about 10 minutes. Brush the sauce over the ribs and broil 1 to 3 minutes or until sizzling.

Make ahead Slow-cook the ribs and keep refrigerated for up to 1 day. Bake at 350°F for 10 minutes, then brush with sauce and broil.

Lemony Lamb Chops

Serves 2 to 3

My grandmother Pauline always included the details of her supper in her long letters. She lived alone in a fabulous downtown Montreal apartment, and frequently recounted that she had enjoyed two lamb chops with a baked potato and some peas—yum! Little T-bone chops, sometimes called loin chops, are usually less expensive than rib chops, which are cut from a rack of lamb. They're very easy and fast to cook, extremely flavourful and tender, and they don't need much to become a lovely weeknight meal. I take my cue from Nana Pauline and usually pair them with Jacket Potatoes (page 184) and Minty Peas (page 178).

....

1. Position one oven rack about 4 inches below the broiler and preheat the broiler. Line a baking pan with foil.

2. Rub the cut side of the garlic over both sides of each lamb chop, then brush with canola oil. Sprinkle with the salt and season with pepper.

3. Broil 5 minutes. Turn the chops and broil another 2 to 5 minutes or until firm to the touch but still springy. They will be cooked to medium; if you prefer them well done, leave them under the broiler for another 3 to 5 minutes.

4. Sprinkle chops with parsley (if using) and serve immediately with lemon wedges.

Prep Time less than 10 minutes
Ready In about 15 minutes

8 lamb T-bone or loin chops

2 large cloves garlic, peeled and cut in half

1 tablespoon canola oil

¼ teaspoon salt

Fresh black pepper

Chopped fresh parsley or mint (optional)

1 lemon, cut into wedges, for garnish

Fish and Seafood

Baked Lemon Salmon

Serves 4 • Make ahead

Prep Time 5 minutes or less
Ready In about 25 minutes

4 skin-on salmon fillets
(5 ounces/150 g each)

½ teaspoon salt

Fresh black pepper

1 small lemon, thinly sliced

Cooking salmon with this method is my solution to all the regular complaints about fish: it won't smell up the whole house, it won't be dried out and it will be full of flavour. The method, called *en papillote*, is a traditional cooking technique usually done with parchment paper, but I find using aluminum foil far easier and less fussy. The foil packet creates a steamy little mini-oven that perfectly cooks the fish and also contains all fishy smells. It's an entirely forgiving technique, too. The packet moderates the oven's heat so it's almost impossible to overcook the fish or lose the moisture. Best of all, clean-up means just balling up the foil and tossing it in the garbage. Basmati rice or boiled potatoes and Sweet-and-Sour Bok Choy (page 179) will complement the salmon nicely.

....

1. Preheat the oven to 375°F. Tear off a very long sheet of foil and place one half of it on a rimmed baking sheet.

2. Place the salmon on that half of the foil, skin side down, leaving about an inch between each fillet. Sprinkle salmon with the salt and season with pepper. Top with lemon slices. Fold over and crimp the foil into a loose packet. There should be lots of air in there.

3. Bake 17 to 20 minutes or until the fish looks completely opaque, and when you press a fillet gently with your finger it springs back. There will be tiny ridges of white protein along the edges of the fish, a sign that the fish is cooked.

4. Open the foil packet and use a thin metal spatula to lift the fillets off the skin, leaving the skin on the foil, and place the fillets on plates.

Make ahead This salmon is equally delicious hot, warm or cold. I often make it up to 1 day ahead and then serve it cold, flaked into a big green salad or in a soft white bun with lots of mayonnaise and Dijon mustard.

British-Style Fish Pie

Serves 4 to 6 • Make ahead

In Britain, fish pie is as common as mac and cheese is in North America. It's a wonderful dish, sort of like shepherd's pie, but with a delicious lemony, creamy mixed-fish filling instead of ground meat. And just like shepherd's pie, there is no pastry here but rather a mashed-potato top crust. British fish pie always contains some smoked fish—usually smoked haddock, which is almost impossible to find in North America. In its place I use hot-smoked trout or salmon (look for it in the seafood counter), but you could also use the tins of boneless smoked herring fillets.

···

1. Preheat the oven to 350°F.

2. To make the Mashed Potatoes, peel potatoes and cut each one into quarters. Place in a large pot and cover with cold water by 1 inch. Add the salt, cover and bring to a boil. Reduce heat and simmer, partially covered, 15 minutes or until very tender. Drain potatoes, then mash or pass through a ricer back into the cooking pot. Stir in the milk and butter. Reserve (it's okay if it gets cold).

3. To make the Creamy Fish Filling, melt the butter in a wide frying pan over medium heat. Add the leeks and cook 5 to 8 minutes or until very soft. Sprinkle in the flour and stir well to combine. Whisk in about half the milk, stirring until the sauce is smooth and thick. Whisk in the rest of the milk and cook gently, stirring occasionally, until thickened, about 3 minutes. Whisk in the cream and salt.

4. Turn off the heat and stir in the peas, parsley and lemon zest. Stir in the fish. Transfer to an 8-cup baking dish and smooth the top. Place the dish on a baking sheet.

5. Dollop the mashed potatoes over the fish mixture and smooth into an even layer. Sprinkle with cheese. Bake 40 minutes or until bubbly at the edges. Let stand 5 minutes before serving.

Tip Cold water shrimp are tiny and usually very sweet and tender. They come already peeled and deveined, and are sold frozen (there's no need to thaw them first).

Make ahead Assemble the pie and refrigerate for up to 12 hours. Bake 50 to 60 minutes or until bubbly at the edges.

Prep Time 30 minutes
Ready In a little over 1 hour

Mashed Potatoes

3 pounds (1.35 kg) Yukon Gold potatoes (about 7 medium potatoes)

1 teaspoon salt

1⅓ cups 2% milk

3 tablespoons butter, at room temperature

Creamy Fish Filling

3 tablespoons butter

2 leeks (white and light green part only), thinly sliced in half-moons

2 tablespoons all-purpose flour

1 cup 2% milk

¼ cup whipping (35%) cream

½ teaspoon salt

1½ cups fresh or frozen peas

½ cup chopped fresh parsley

Zest of 1 lemon

8 ounces (225 g) skinless salmon fillet, cubed

5 ounces (150 g) cold water shrimp (see Tip)

5 ounces (150 g) hot-smoked salmon, flaked

1 cup grated old white Cheddar cheese

Broiled Miso Salmon

Serves 2 • Make ahead

Prep Time 5 minutes or less
Ready In about ½ hour

2 tablespoons white or red miso paste (see Tip on page 44)

2 tablespoons dry white wine or dry vermouth

1 tablespoon pure maple syrup

2 skin-on salmon fillets (6 ounces/170 g each)

This is one of my favourite ways to cook fish. It's inspired by a classic Japanese restaurant treatment for any rich fish (usually black cod), but it's made simpler and more North American with maple syrup instead of mirin. The combination of salty miso with sweet syrup and fragrant wine is simply unbeatable—not to mention easy. Under the broiler the salmon gets a little crispy on top but stays wonderfully moist and delicious. This is so special-tasting that I often serve it for an at-home date night, and you can easily double or triple the recipe if company's coming. I usually serve this salmon with basmati rice and Sweet-and-Sour Bok Choy (page 179) or green beans sautéed with sesame seeds.

1. Whisk the miso, white wine and maple syrup together in a shallow dish. Add the salmon, skin side up. Let stand at room temperature for 20 minutes.

2. Meanwhile, position one oven rack about 4 inches below the broiler and preheat the broiler. Line a rimmed baking sheet with foil.

3. Lift the fish from the marinade and place skin side down on the prepared baking sheet. Broil 10 minutes or until the top edges are deep golden and the fish flakes easily when pressed with a fork. Use a thin metal spatula to lift the fillets off the skin, leaving the skin on the foil, and place on plates. Serve immediately.

Make ahead Marinate the salmon for up to 24 hours in the fridge.

Lemon and Herb Salmon Loaf

Serves 4 • Make ahead

This is one of my favourite dishes in this book. It's delicious, easy, inexpensive—the gold standard of uncomplicated. It's also such a clever and quick way to get more fish into our diets. I first tasted salmon loaf in Nova Scotia, made by a friend's mom who is frugal and smart in the kitchen. I'd never liked canned salmon, but after that first taste I started buying a can with every week's shopping, and now salmon loaf is one of our weekday regulars. The parsley and lemon really brighten the dish. Serve with a hearty vegetable side dish like Curry-Spiced Roasted Squash (page 188) or Grilled Corn (page 185).

Prep Time 15 minutes
Ready In about 1 hour

2 eggs

1 cup 2% milk

2 cans (8 ounces/213 g each) salmon, drained (see Tip)

1½ cups panko crumbs

1 yellow onion, very finely chopped

½ cup chopped fresh parsley or dill

Zest of 1 lemon

2 tablespoons fresh lemon juice

¾ teaspoon salt

1 teaspoon butter

Sour cream (optional)

1. Preheat the oven to 350°F. Generously grease an 8- x 4-inch loaf pan with non-stick cooking spray.

2. Whisk the eggs and milk together in a large bowl. Add the salmon and mash it up with a fork. Add the panko, onion, parsley, lemon zest and juice, and salt and stir very well to combine. Scrape into the prepared pan and pack it down firmly. Smooth the top. Cut the butter into little bits and sprinkle evenly over the loaf.

3. Bake 50 to 55 minutes or until golden on top and a small sharp knife inserted into the centre of the loaf comes out feeling hot to the touch. Slice and serve with a dollop of sour cream, if using.

Tip Canned salmon is almost always wild-caught. It is often packed with its skin and bones, which become completely soft during processing. Mash the skin and bones into the dish and they'll boost the calcium content significantly (and trust me, no one will ever know). Alternatively, you can buy boneless, skinless canned salmon.

Make ahead Assemble the salmon mixture and keep chilled for up to 12 hours before transferring to the loaf pan and cooking. Add 10 to 15 minutes to the cooking time.

Thai Shrimp Curry

Serves 4

Prep Time 15 minutes
Ready In about ½ hour

1 cup chicken broth

1 can (14 ounces/400 mL)
full-fat coconut milk

3 tablespoons Thai red curry
paste

2 small Japanese eggplants,
cut in ½-inch half-moons

1 small head broccoli, cut into
small florets

12 ounces (340 g) peeled
and deveined medium
shrimp (26 to 30 count;
see Tip page 123)

Zest of 1 lime

2 tablespoons fresh lime juice

2 to 3 teaspoons fish sauce

Chopped fresh cilantro,
for garnish

Thai curries are a great favourite in our house, but they can be complicated to make from scratch. I wanted to create a recipe that was more straightforward, so instead of making my own curry paste, I use the jarred kind, which I find to be just as delicious. As well, instead of starting the recipe with lots of sautéing, I just add ingredients to a simmering broth. It makes the curry very saucy, and perfect for serving over a bowl of steamed rice.

1. Whisk broth and coconut milk together in a medium saucepan. Whisk in the curry paste. Bring to a simmer over medium heat.

2. Add the eggplant, bring to a boil, then reduce heat and simmer, stirring occasionally, 10 to 15 minutes or until the eggplant is tender. Add broccoli and simmer another 1 minute. Add shrimp and simmer 1 to 3 minutes or until they are just cooked.

3. Remove from the heat and stir in lime zest, lime juice and fish sauce (start with 2 teaspoons and add another if you like). Divide among 4 bowls and garnish with cilantro.

Tip Japanese eggplants are long and slender, and have a much smoother texture than their large Italian siblings. They are getting easier to find in supermarkets, but if you can't get them, use about 20 button mushrooms, sliced, instead.

Switch it up Use sliced chicken or firm tofu in place of the shrimp. Add chicken about 3 minutes before adding the broccoli. Tofu can be added at the same time shrimp would be added.

Grilled Chili-Lime Shrimp

Serves 4 • Make ahead

Shrimp are naturally sweet and tender, and I find the trick to keeping them that way is to cook them in the shell. But to help the shrimp take in this yummy marinade, I use deveined shrimp, which are split down the back. Shrimp are sold according to their size (the "count" number refers to how many of that size are in one pound) and you can usually find them already deveined. These are delicious served as an appetizer, or as supper alongside Sweet-and-Sour Bok Choy (page 179) and Grilled Corn (page 185). You could also use these in place of tofu in Chilled Cucumber and Sesame Noodles with Tofu (page 161).

Prep Time 5 minutes or less
Ready In about ½ hour

12 ounces (340 g) shell-on extra-large shrimp (18 to 20 count), deveined

¼ cup dry vermouth or dry white wine

1 teaspoon sesame oil

¼ cup fresh lime juice

1 teaspoon hot chili-garlic sauce

1. Stir the shrimp with the vermouth and sesame oil in a medium bowl. Let stand at room temperature for 20 minutes. Meanwhile, soak 4 long bamboo skewers in water.

2. Preheat the grill to high. Thread the shrimp onto the skewers.

3. Grill skewers, with the lid closed, 1 to 2 minutes per side or until the shrimp are bright pink and just cooked through. Transfer skewers to a platter. (Take the shrimp off the skewers if you wish.)

4. Stir the lime juice and chili-garlic sauce together in a small bowl, then brush over the shrimp.

Tip To devein shrimp, with a sharp paring knife, make a shallow cut down the back of the shrimp, starting at the head (or open) end and stopping just before the tail. Remove and discard the grey or pink vein.

Make ahead Marinate the shrimp for up to 1 day in the fridge. I usually toss them into the marinade when they are frozen and let them thaw right in there.

Broiled Fish with Maître d' Butter

Serves 4 • Make ahead

Prep Time 10 minutes
Ready In about 20 minutes

3 tablespoons butter, at room temperature

1 clove garlic, grated

½ small shallot, finely minced

2 tablespoons fresh lemon juice

2 tablespoons finely chopped fresh parsley

1 tablespoon canola oil

½ teaspoon salt

4 skin-on white fish fillets (5 ounces/150 g each; see Tip)

When I eat in nice restaurants I usually order fish. Chefs source the freshest fish and cook it marvellously, so the skin is crispy but the flesh is moist. To replicate that experience at home, I buy two small whole fish and ask the fish shop to fillet them for me. I cook the fish in a really hot pan so the skin gets crispy, but because fillets can be tricky to flip over, I finish cooking them in the oven (no flipping required). Maître d' (or maître d'hôtel) is a type of compound butter; it's an easy restaurant trick for adding tons of flavour. Here it acts like an instant sauce, making the whole dish so yummy that it feels like eating out. Serve with Celery and Fennel Salad (page 178) and boiled or Jacket Potatoes (page 184).

1. Position one oven rack about 4 inches below the broiler and preheat the broiler.

2. To make the compound butter, mash the butter, garlic and shallot together well with a fork in a small bowl. Gradually mash in the lemon juice, then add the parsley, stirring gently so it doesn't turn the butter green.

3. Heat an oven-safe frying pan over high heat. Once it's really hot, add the canola oil. Sprinkle salt over both sides of the fish, then carefully place the fillets skin side down in the pan. Cook 2 to 3 minutes, without touching them, or until the flesh closest to the skin is just cooked and opaque.

4. Transfer the pan to the oven and broil 2 to 4 minutes or until the fish is just barely cooked through.

5. Place about 1 tablespoon of compound butter on each fillet, then broil another 30 seconds or until the butter melts.

6. Use a thin metal spatula to separate the fish skin from the pan. Serve immediately (and don't forget to eat the skin—I think it's the best part!)

Tip Look for any mild, semi-firm, skin-on white fish fillets, such as sea bream, catfish, branzino or red snapper. Each fillet should be between ½ and ¾ inches thick.

Make ahead Make the compound butter up to 1 day in advance. Dollop it onto a piece of plastic wrap and roll it into a cylinder, then chill. It's also delicious on salmon, chicken and vegetables.

Crunchy Fish Tacos

Serves 4 • Make ahead

Prep Time 20 minutes or less
Ready In about 40 minutes

2 tablespoons all-purpose flour

Fresh black pepper

1 egg

1½ cups crushed salted saltine crackers (¾ sleeve)

1 pound (450 g) tilapia fillets (or another skinless white fish, such as catfish or haddock)

4 teaspoons canola oil

3 cups coleslaw mix (about half a 14-ounce/397 g bag)

½ cup chopped fresh cilantro

3 tablespoons fresh lime juice

¼ teaspoon salt

8 small soft tortillas

2 tomatoes, chopped

1 avocado, pitted and sliced

Sliced fresh jalapeño pepper (optional)

Sour cream (optional)

Fish tacos are such a fun way to eat fish. Most restaurants batter and fry their fish, but since I'm not a fan of deep-frying at home, I like this baked version even better. The crushed cracker crust gives the fish great texture. You can use frozen fish for this recipe, but thaw it completely, and dry it really well before adding the crust. Coleslaw mix speeds up prep time enough to make these a good weeknight supper. This is a one-dish meal for us, since it's protein, starch and lots of veggies all at once.

....

1. Preheat the oven to 450°F. Line a rimmed baking sheet with foil.

2. Place the flour in a shallow bowl and season with pepper. Beat the egg lightly in a second shallow bowl. Place crushed saltines in a third bowl. Pat the fish dry with paper towel, then dip it into the flour, coating it all over. Shake off the excess, then dip the fish into the egg. Let the excess drip off, then place the fish in the crushed saltines and press the crumbs into both sides of the fish.

3. Transfer the fish to the prepared baking sheet. Drizzle each fillet with 1 teaspoon canola oil. Bake 10 to 12 minutes or until bubbly at the edges and cooked through.

4. Meanwhile, stir the coleslaw mix with cilantro, lime juice and salt in a large bowl. Warm the tortillas according to package directions.

5. Gently break the cooked fish into large flakes. Divide among tortillas and top with coleslaw, tomatoes, avocado, and jalapeño and sour cream, if using.

Tip To crush the saltines easily, put them in a resealable plastic bag and crush them with a rolling pin or other heavy implement.

Make ahead The coleslaw mixture can sit for up to 3 hours in the fridge. It's also tasty on its own, or served with Slow-Cooker Sweet and Spicy Ribs (page 106) or Lemon and Spice Grilled Chicken (page 79).

No-Cook Summer Tuna

Serves 2 • Make ahead

Prep Time 15 minutes
Ready In about 15 minutes

½ shallot, minced

3 tablespoons red wine vinegar

3 tablespoons extra-virgin olive oil

¼ teaspoon salt

¼ cup chopped fresh parsley

1 can (19 ounces/540 mL) white kidney beans, drained and rinsed

1 pint mixed cherry tomatoes, halved

3 cans (3 ounces/80 g each) olive-oil-packed tuna (see Tip on page 40)

1 avocado, pitted and sliced

Chopped fresh chives, for garnish

On those hot and humid summer evenings when turning on the stove or oven is unthinkable, I turn to this dish. Part salad, part antipasto platter, it's refreshing and satisfying and requires no cooking. I also love using pantry ingredients like tuna and beans in a way that elevates them to dinner status, although leftovers of this dish make a wonderful packed lunch the next day. Thanks to good-quality greenhouse cherry tomatoes, you can also make this in the middle of winter and get a little taste of early August. Serve with good bread, or even with a simple pasta dish such as Garlic Spaghetti (page 170).

....

1. Combine shallots and red wine vinegar in a large bowl. Let stand 10 minutes.

2. Stir in the olive oil, salt and parsley, then add beans and tomatoes and mix well.

3. Gently fold in the tuna and avocado. Garnish with chives.

Tip Shallots are in the onion family. They are much milder than onions, and have a faint garlic flavour. They're distinctive and delicious, and the other half you don't need here can be used in a batch of Maître d' Butter (see page 124). If you don't have any shallots, use 2 small green onions instead.

Make ahead Finish the recipe to the end of step 2 and refrigerate for up to 1 day. Stir in the tuna and avocado just before serving.

Vegetarian

Vegetable Pizza

Serves 4 • Make ahead

Prep Time about 15 minutes
Ready In about 20 minutes if
dough is ready

3¾ cups (575 g) all-purpose
flour

1 teaspoon salt

¼ teaspoon active dry yeast

1½ cups cool water

1 can (28 ounces/796 mL)
whole tomatoes

¼ teaspoon salt

3 cups shredded mozzarella
cheese

Thinly sliced yellow onion

1 bunch thin asparagus

Fresh thyme leaves

Make ahead Make the
dough up to 36 hours ahead
of time (leave it on the
counter for the whole time).
Make the tomato sauce up
to 2 days in advance and
keep refrigerated.

Switch it up I like to use
a mix of all-purpose and
whole wheat flours for the
dough, preferably about
2 cups (300 g) all-purpose
plus 1½ cups (275 g)
whole wheat.

Sometimes you just want to lie on the couch and eat pizza out of a box. And
that's cool. But when you want to make it yourself, I've got great news: it can
be so easy—no baking stone or dough-tossing required.

In our house, we eat pizza almost every Friday night. Determined to
make the process as easy as possible, I tweaked my dough and sauce recipes
relentlessly. Once the dough and sauce work, you can use whatever toppings
you like. Yes, you need to start the no-knead, slow-rise dough at least 12 hours
before you plan to cook it, but I've stirred it up while tipsy with only one eye
open and even once in the middle of the night when I couldn't sleep, so trust
me, you can do it any time. We tend to keep our pizzas vegetarian, but you
can add anything you like. Serve this with a large green salad.

1. At least 12 hours before pizza time, make the dough. Stir the flour, salt and
yeast together in a large bowl. Stir in the water until it's well incorporated. It
should look sticky. Cover the bowl and leave it alone on the counter for at
least 12 hours.

2. Preheat the oven to 450°F. Pour the tomatoes into a fine-mesh sieve set over
a bowl. Crush them a bit, and let them drain while you roll out the dough.

3. Grease a large rimmed baking sheet, paying special attention to the corners.
Generously sprinkle the counter with flour, then scrape the dough onto the
counter. The dough will be wobbly. Sprinkle the top generously with flour. Pull
and press the dough into roughly the shape of your pan. Transfer it to the pan
and continue to press, squish and pull it into shape so that it fills the entire sheet.

4. Reserve or discard the tomato liquid, then transfer the drained tomatoes
into the bowl. Add the salt and smash and crush them with your hands.
Spread the sauce all over the dough. Top with mozzarella cheese, onion,
asparagus and thyme (or whatever toppings you like).

5. Bake 15 to 20 minutes or until the mozzarella is bubbly and golden
brown. Let stand 5 minutes before cutting and serving.

Tip This dough recipe makes about 2 pounds (900 g). To use it for
Grilled Barbecue Chicken Pizza (page 85), either halve the recipe or
make the whole recipe and store half the risen dough in a resealable plastic
bag in the freezer for up to 1 month. Thaw it in the fridge, then roll it out.

Double Portobello Cheeseburgers

Serves 4

One of my dearest foodie friends, Sasha, is a former restaurant chef and a genius in the kitchen. We've had many extraordinary meals at her table, but the mushroom burgers she threw together one weeknight really stuck with me. She grilled big portobellos and topped them with about four different types of cheese, then served them stacked two-up in buns like outrageous hamburgers. But instead of feeling overstuffed, as I would after a double hamburger, I felt great! I like that this is a playful recipe, too, because the grilled mushrooms look just like meat patties.

Instead of using many different cheeses, I like to add some garlic butter and just use the Cheddar we always have in the fridge. These don't need any additional condiments except maybe a smear of grainy Dijon mustard. Serve with Celery and Fennel Salad (page 178) or any crunchy green slaw.

Prep Time 15 minutes
Ready In about ½ hour

1 large clove garlic, finely minced

2 tablespoons butter, at room temperature

2 tablespoons chopped fresh parsley

8 portobello mushrooms

1½ cups grated old Cheddar cheese

4 burger buns

....

1. Preheat the grill to high.

2. Mash the garlic with the butter and parsley in a small bowl.

3. Remove and discard the mushroom stems, then use a small spoon to scrape out and discard the dark brown gills from the underside of the mushrooms.

4. Place mushrooms stem side down on the grill. Close the lid and cook 5 minutes. Reduce heat to low, turn the mushrooms stem side up and smear them with the butter mixture. Cook, with the lid closed, another 4 to 8 minutes or until the mushrooms are tender.

5. Sprinkle with cheese and cook, with the lid closed, until the cheese melts. Stack 2 mushrooms on each bun.

Tip A mushroom's "gills" are the feathery soft parts right under the cap. In portobellos they are very dark brown and tend to turn any other food close to them an unappetizing dark grey colour. They're also mostly water and slow down the grilling process.

Ricotta Dumplings

Serves 3 to 4 • Make ahead

Prep Time 20 minutes
Ready In about 25 minutes

3 eggs

2 cups ricotta cheese (about 15 ounces/425 g)

1 cup all-purpose flour

1½ teaspoons salt

2 cups Uncomplicated Tomato Sauce (page 162) or store-bought marinara sauce, warmed

For garnish

Extra-virgin olive oil

Grated Parmesan cheese

Chopped fresh parsley or chives

I love homemade ravioli, but since making them by hand takes most of an afternoon, I often whip up these dumplings as an easy weeknight substitute. The three-ingredient mixture is so quick to assemble, and the resulting dumplings are light, fluffy and satisfying. Cooking the dumplings in barely simmering water is the key to getting the texture just right. You can serve them tossed in melted butter, but I like a little simple tomato sauce on top even better. I serve these with a big green salad such as Supper Salad (page 47).

1. Preheat the oven to 300°F. Bring a large, wide pot of salted water to a boil; reduce heat to a gentle simmer. Line a large rimmed baking sheet with parchment paper or foil.

2. Whisk the eggs in a large bowl, then whisk in the ricotta, then the flour and salt.

3. Use two cereal spoons to drop large blobs of batter into the gently simmering water (use one spoon to hold the batter and the other spoon to scrape the batter into the water). You will need to do this in two batches.

4. Simmer dumplings 5 minutes or until firm and cooked through. Use a slotted spoon to lift them out of the water and place them on the prepared baking sheet. Keep the first batch warm in the oven while you cook the second batch.

5. Serve with Uncomplicated Tomato Sauce and garnish with a drizzle of olive oil, some Parmesan and parsley.

Make ahead Cook the dumplings, then cool them on a baking sheet lined with parchment paper. Store in a single layer in an airtight container in the fridge for up to 1 day. Reheat by plunging into simmering water for 1 minute.

Soy-Ginger Tofu

Serves 3 to 4 • Make ahead

I call this "gateway tofu" because it has converted many tofu haters. The saltiness of the soy sauce mixed with zesty ginger and rich sesame oil transforms humble tofu into an exceptionally tasty dish. It's terrific on its own, served with rice and vegetables, or added to soups or stir-fries. For a delicious supper I like to add saucy stir-fried greens like my Sweet-and-Sour Bok Choy (page 179) plus some basmati or brown rice.

....

1. Preheat the oven to 400°F.

2. Cut the tofu into 6 slices. Stir the soy sauce, sesame oil, ginger and chili-garlic sauce (if using) in a shallow 8-inch square baking dish. Add the tofu slices and marinate for 15 minutes, turning over the slices halfway through.

3. Transfer the dish to the oven and bake 15 minutes or until the tofu is piping hot.

Make ahead Marinate the tofu in the fridge for up to 24 hours.

Prep Time 10 minutes or less
Ready In a little over ½ hour

1 pound (450 g) medium or firm tofu

3 tablespoons soy sauce

2 teaspoons sesame oil

1 teaspoon grated fresh ginger

1 teaspoon hot chili-garlic sauce (optional)

Fresh Vegetable Chili

Serves 4 • Make ahead

Prep Time 20 minutes
Ready In about 45 minutes

2 tablespoons canola oil

1 yellow onion, chopped

½ teaspoon salt

1 carrot, chopped

1 stalk celery, chopped

1 sweet red pepper, chopped

1 zucchini, chopped

3 cloves garlic, minced

4 teaspoons chili powder

1 teaspoon ground cumin

1 can (28 ounces/796 mL) whole tomatoes, crushed up a bit

1 can (5.5 ounces/156 mL) tomato paste

1 can (19 ounces/540 mL) kidney beans, drained and rinsed

1 cup frozen or canned corn kernels

½ cup dry white wine

¼ cup chopped fresh parsley

For garnish

Sour cream

Grated Cheddar cheese

Sliced avocado

This is a recipe I often make on a Monday so my family and I can enjoy it for lunches all week long. Because the recipe focuses on vegetables (instead of beans or meat substitutes), it has a freshness that keeps it from getting boring, and I love the different colours and textures. When chopping the vegetables, I try to make them all about the same size. This makes the chili more visually appealing and somehow more delicious. Whole canned tomatoes, crushed up a bit, are much more flavourful than the pre-diced ones.

This dish doesn't need anything extra, but to make it a little heartier, serve it spooned over Jacket Potatoes (page 184) or rice.

1. Heat the canola oil in a large pot over medium heat. Add the onion and salt and cook, stirring occasionally, 3 to 4 minutes or until softened and slightly golden. Add the carrot and celery and cook 2 minutes or until starting to soften. Stir in the red pepper, zucchini and garlic and cook 1 minute or so. Stir in chili powder and cumin and cook 30 seconds.

2. Add tomatoes with their juices and tomato paste and bring to a boil. Reduce heat to low, cover and simmer, stirring occasionally, 10 to 15 minutes or until the zucchini and peppers are just tender.

3. Stir in beans, corn, white wine and parsley and simmer another 5 minutes.

4. Serve garnished with sour cream, Cheddar and avocado.

Tip There are two easy ways to crush whole tomatoes. Use a pair of kitchen scissors to snip them up in the can, or pour some of the juice out into the pot and then use your hand to crush each tomato before adding to the pot.

Make ahead This keeps well in the fridge for up to 3 days. I find it doesn't freeze well—the vegetables get too mushy.

Mushroom and Asparagus Frittata

Serves 4 • Make ahead

This could be called "Whatever Is in the Fridge" Frittata because it's so
flexible. As long as it's got onions, eggs and cheese, this is a delicious supper,
lunch or breakfast—and it makes for excellent leftovers, too. It might seem
a little fussy because it needs to be started on the stove and then moved to
the oven, but it's actually easy and fast. To add a bit more to the meal, serve
Jacket Potatoes (page 184) or Curry-Spiced Roasted Squash (page 188).

Prep Time 10 minutes or less
Ready In about 20 minutes

8 eggs

¼ cup 2% milk or whipping
(35%) cream

¾ teaspoon salt, divided

2 tablespoons canola oil,
divided

1 medium yellow onion, thinly
sliced

6 button or cremini
mushrooms, sliced

6 spears of asparagus,
trimmed and cut into 2-inch
lengths

4 ounces (115 g) plain soft
goat cheese (about ⅓ cup)

Fresh black pepper

1. Preheat the oven to 350°F.

2. Whisk the eggs with the milk and ½ teaspoon of the salt in a medium
bowl. Reserve.

3. Heat an 8- or 10-inch oven-safe frying pan over medium-high heat. Add
1 tablespoon of the canola oil. Add the onion and remaining ¼ teaspoon
salt. Cook, stirring often, 2 minutes. Add the mushrooms and cook, stirring
often, another 5 minutes or until mushrooms are golden and tender. Add
the asparagus and cook another 1 to 2 minutes or until tender-crisp.

4. Reduce heat to medium. Drizzle the remaining 1 tablespoon canola oil
over the vegetables and spread them into an even layer. Pour the egg
mixture over top. Break the goat cheese into small lumps and sprinkle
evenly over the egg. Season with pepper. Cook 1 to 2 minutes or until you
can see one or two bubbling spots in the egg mixture. Transfer to the oven.

5. Bake 5 minutes. Switch on the broiler and set the timer for 2 minutes.
After 2 minutes the frittata should be set but still jiggly (it will continue
to cook after it comes out of the oven). If it's still wet, continue to broil,
checking every 30 seconds or so. Remove from the oven and let stand
5 minutes before serving.

Make ahead Make the frittata up to 1 day in advance and keep it, well
wrapped in plastic, in the fridge. Reheat on medium in the microwave,
or serve cold.

Switch it up Instead of mushrooms and asparagus, use any combination of
sliced peppers, diced zucchini, baby spinach, sliced tomatoes or broccoli
florets. You can also add 2 tablespoons of chopped fresh parsley, dill, chives
or basil. In place of the goat cheese, use ricotta or feta.

Easy Cheddar Soufflé

Serves 3 to 4 • Make ahead

Prep Time 20 minutes
Ready In a little over 1 hour

6 eggs

⅓ cup butter

⅓ cup all-purpose flour

1 teaspoon Dijon mustard

⅛ teaspoon cayenne
(optional)

1½ cups 2% milk

1½ cups finely diced old
Cheddar cheese (about
6 ounces/170 g)

¼ teaspoon salt

Make ahead Separate the
eggs and make the cheese
sauce. Keep the sauce at
room temperature for up to
2 hours or in the fridge for
up to 24 hours. Just before
cooking, whip egg whites.
Whisk the cheese sauce
very well to loosen it, then
incorporate the egg whites
and cheese sauce as per
the recipe.

Soufflé sounds fancy and, by extension, complicated, but if you can separate eggs, you can make soufflé. Its pillowy-soft interior and crisp, cheesy crust make it extraordinarily comforting, but it's also a dazzling dish to bring out of the oven for company. I have often made this for visiting family, and they always request it the next time they're in town. It does need to be served the moment it comes out of the oven, so make sure to have the table set and everyone sitting down just before the timer goes off. Any sweet-sour chutney goes well with this soufflé, including ketchup. Serve with Minty Peas (page 178) or a large green salad.

1. Preheat the oven to 350°F. Butter a 1.5 L soufflé dish or 5-inch-deep straight-sided baking dish.

2. Separate the eggs, placing the whites in the bowl of an electric mixer (or a large mixing bowl) and the yolks in a small bowl. If any yolk gets in with the whites, scoop it out with half an eggshell, but don't worry if there's a little white in with the yolks. Set aside.

3. Melt the butter in a medium saucepan over medium heat. Whisk in the flour until combined. Whisk in the mustard and cayenne, if using. Cook, whisking occasionally, 30 seconds. Whisk in the milk and cook, whisking constantly, until thickened, about 2 minutes. About halfway through, switch from a whisk to a silicone or rubber spatula, making sure to scrape along the bottom and sides of the pot.

4. Add the cheese and salt and stir until the cheese is melted. Remove from the heat. Whisk the egg yolks with a fork until well combined, then stir into the cheese mixture. Let cool for at least 15 minutes.

5. Whip the egg whites on high until they hold soft peaks, 1 to 2 minutes. When you pull the whisk out of the mixture and hold it upside down, the whites should hold a floppy peak shape. Pour the cheese mixture into the egg whites and fold gently but thoroughly until there are no more clumps of white.

6. Pour gently into the prepared dish. Bake until very puffy and golden, 35 to 40 minutes. Serve immediately.

Saucy Tex-Mex Black Beans

Serves 4 • Make ahead

When I lived alone, my cooking took a lot of inspiration from a book of essays called *Alone in the Kitchen with an Eggplant*. In this anthology, writers from various fields of expertise described what and how they ate while alone. The essays were fascinating, liberating and gave me lots of great ideas. Jeremy Jackson's essay, "Beans and Me," describes his enduring love for simply cooked black beans, which inspired me to create my own version of a one-pot black bean supper.

Jackson eats his black beans with cornbread, which I do, too, when I can buy it; otherwise, I serve this over rice. Ironically, although I discovered this dish in a book about being single, it's one of my partner Michael's favourites. Serve this on its own, or ladle it over cornbread or basmati rice and serve some Carrot-Lemon Slaw (page 189) alongside.

....

1. Heat the canola oil in a small pot over medium heat. Add the onion and salt and cook, stirring occasionally, about 5 minutes or until softened. Add garlic and cook another minute. Stir in chili powder and cumin and cook 30 seconds. Add the beans and water. Bring to a boil, then reduce heat and simmer, stirring often, 10 minutes or until thickened a little.

2. Purée partially with an immersion blender. (I like to leave some whole black beans intact for texture.) Serve topped with Cheddar, salsa and avocado.

Make ahead This dish keeps well in the fridge for up to 1 day.

Prep Time 10 minutes
Ready In about 20 minutes

1 tablespoon canola oil

1 yellow onion, finely chopped

½ teaspoon salt

4 cloves garlic, minced

2 tablespoons chili powder

2 teaspoons ground cumin

2 cans (19 ounces/540 mL each) black beans, drained and rinsed

1 cup water

Toppings

1 cup grated Cheddar cheese

Fresh Tomato and Corn Salsa (page 209) or store-bought salsa

1 avocado, pitted and sliced

Zucchini-Cheddar Quesadillas

Serves 4

Prep Time 10 minutes
Ready In about 15 minutes

1 medium zucchini

¼ teaspoon salt

Canola oil

8 small soft tortillas

½ small yellow onion, thinly sliced

1 cup grated Cheddar cheese

1 cup shredded mozzarella cheese

For serving

Fresh Tomato and Corn Salsa (page 209) or store-bought salsa

Sour cream

My family's fall-back weeknight meal is quesadillas. I keep tortillas in the freezer and there is always cheese in the fridge, so even when we are time-strapped and the pantry is almost bare, we can have a humble but satisfying meal. One day while grating the cheese for a round of quesadillas, I also grated a small zucchini into the mix, and they turned out better than ever. The zucchini offers a hit of nutrients and fibre without any sacrifice to the flavour or appearance. These are great on their own, served with salsa, or alongside a soup like Split Pea, Butternut and Bacon Soup (page 51).

1. Preheat oven to 300°F.

2. Grate the zucchini on the large holes of a box grater. Place in a colander over a bowl and sprinkle with salt. Give it a little toss to mix in the salt. Let stand 10 minutes, then squeeze as much of the liquid out of the zucchini as possible.

3. Heat a large non-stick frying pan over medium heat. Brush with a tiny bit of canola oil, then place a tortilla in the pan. Sprinkle with one-quarter of the onion and one-quarter of the squeezed zucchini (fluff up the zucchini a bit to get better coverage). Sprinkle evenly with ¼ cup of each cheese. Top with another tortilla and press down with a spatula. Cook 1 minute or until the bottom is golden, then flip and cook another 1 minute or so. Transfer the completed quesadilla to a baking sheet and keep warm in the oven for up to 15 minutes.

4. Repeat with remaining ingredients. Serve with Fresh Tomato and Corn Salsa and sour cream.

Switch it up Add anything you like. I love adding black beans, shredded cooked chicken or beef, grilled sweet peppers or hot sauce.

Simple Nepali Dal

Serves 4 • Make ahead • Slow cooker • Batch cooking

People are usually surprised to hear that I was an extremely picky eater until my twenties. I ate no fish, few eggs and barely any meat. Thankfully, my family discovered lentils when we lived in Nepal in the 1980s. We all fell hard for the glorious marriage of rice and curried lentils, *dal bhat*, that sustains the entire nation (and India, among others). Cheap, fast, nutritious and endlessly interesting, *dal bhat* is still my ultimate comfort food. This version might seem plain, but it's magical, delicious and deeply satisfying. It's possibly the dish I have eaten the most in my life, and I love it just as much today as I ever have. It's great by itself, or serve with some Carrot-Lemon Slaw (page 189) or Lemony Broiled Asparagus (page 182).

Prep Time 5 minutes or less
Ready In about 45 minutes

1½ cups red lentils

2 tablespoons curry powder

6 cups water

1½ teaspoons salt

Cooked basmati rice

Fresh cilantro leaves, for garnish

....

1. Combine the lentils, curry powder and water in a medium pot. Bring to a boil. Lentils take forever to come to a boil but then boil over in a heartbeat, so don't leave them unattended. Once it boils, reduce heat to low and simmer, covered and stirring often, 35 to 40 minutes or until the lentils have completely broken down to a soupy paste.

2. Stir in salt and taste for seasoning. Serve over rice and garnish with cilantro.

Make ahead The dal lasts well in the fridge for up to 1 day, or frozen for up to 2 months.

Slow cooker Combine lentils, curry powder and 5 cups water in the slow cooker. Cover and cook on low for 8 hours. Depending on the cooker, the dal may now need to be cooked on high, uncovered, for about 15 minutes so it becomes a soupy paste. Continue as above.

Batch cooking Cool dal completely, then freeze in 1-cup portions for up to 1 month. You can also tuck ½ cup cooked rice into each container to make it a full meal.

Chickpea and Cauliflower Curry

Serves 4 • Make ahead

Prep Time 15 minutes
Ready In about ½ hour

2 tablespoons canola oil

1 small yellow onion, chopped

½ teaspoon salt

2 cloves garlic, chopped

1 tablespoon minced fresh ginger

1½ teaspoons ground coriander

½ teaspoon turmeric

1 can (5.5 ounces/156 mL) tomato paste

2 cups water

4 cups medium cauliflower florets (about 1 small cauliflower)

1 can (19 ounces/540 mL) chickpeas, drained and rinsed

Plain yogurt (preferably 6%, but at least 2%), for garnish

Fresh cilantro leaves, for garnish

Indian vegetarian recipes are some of the best meatless dishes in the world. The flavours and textures of a vegetable curry are complex and multi-layered, but that doesn't mean they take a lot of time or effort. Here, the simple combination of garlic, ginger and coriander gets a boost from earthy turmeric and tangy tomato to make a wonderful sauce for cauliflower, while chickpeas add heft and protein. I also really love the dish's gorgeous dark orange colour. Serve with basmati rice.

....

1. Heat the canola oil in a large pot over medium heat. Add the onion and salt and cook, stirring occasionally, 5 minutes or until softened.

2. Add garlic and ginger and cook 2 minutes or until everything is lightly golden. Stir in coriander and turmeric and cook 30 seconds.

3. Stir in the tomato paste, then gradually add the water. Bring to a boil, then add cauliflower. Stir well, reduce heat, cover and simmer gently 5 minutes or until the cauliflower is just fork-tender. Stir in the chickpeas and cook 1 minute. Serve topped with a big dollop of yogurt and some fresh cilantro.

Make ahead The curry keeps well for up to 24 hours in the fridge. If you're making it ahead, undercook the cauliflower by about 3 minutes; it will finish cooking while the curry reheats.

Pasta

Tomato and Brie Pasta

Serves 2 to 3

This dish makes an appearance annually for my sister's birthday celebration in mid-summer, when local tomatoes and basil are at their peak, but because I crave it all year long, I had to figure out a way to make it with winter tomatoes. The solution is to use the sweetest, juiciest greenhouse cherry tomatoes you can find and add them right before serving.

This is a luxurious dish, as the Brie melts and coats the pasta and forms a kind of pseudo-sauce, but the tomatoes and basil brighten it up. For a bigger meal, it would go well with Maple-Garlic Cedar Salmon (page 232) or Green Goddess Salad (page 43).

··

1. Boil linguine in a large pot of salted water until just tender, about 10 minutes or according to package directions.

2. Meanwhile, trim off and discard the rind from the Brie. Tear Brie into pieces the size of large peas and place in a large bowl. Drizzle with 2 tablespoons of the olive oil. In a small bowl, combine tomatoes with garlic and salt; let stand at least 10 minutes.

3. Scoop out about ¼ cup of the pasta cooking water, then drain the pasta and immediately add it to the Brie. Toss and stir, then add 2 tablespoons of the pasta cooking water and stir until the Brie is mostly melted.

4. Add the remaining 2 tablespoons pasta cooking water to the tomato mixture along with the remaining 2 tablespoons olive oil.

5. Divide the linguine among 2 or 3 warmed bowls (see Tip) and top with the tomato mixture. Garnish with basil and pepper. Serve immediately.

Tip 1. Use a wedge of Brie cut from a large wheel; the bigger wheels are creamier than the small ones. 2. Serving any pasta in warmed bowls is an easy upgrade. Just ladle a little pasta cooking water into each bowl before draining the pasta, then empty out the bowls before serving up the pasta.

Switch it up When home-grown or vine-ripened tomatoes are in season, chop them coarsely and use in place of cherry tomatoes. Double the basil and salt.

Prep Time 10 minutes
Ready In about 25 minutes

8 ounces (225 g) linguine

7 ounces (200 g) Brie cheese (see Tip)

¼ cup extra-virgin olive oil, divided

1 package (8 ounces/225 g) cherry tomatoes, cut in half (about 1½ cups)

1 small clove garlic, grated or minced

¼ teaspoon salt

¼ cup torn fresh basil leaves

Fresh black pepper

Pasta Carbonara

Serves 2 to 3

Prep Time 10 minutes or less
Ready In about 20 minutes

8 ounces (225 g) linguine or
other spaghetti

4 strips bacon

¼ teaspoon hot chili flakes
(optional)

2 egg yolks

2 tablespoons whipping (35%)
cream

½ cup finely grated Parmesan
cheese, plus more for serving

¼ teaspoon salt

Fresh black pepper

Every cook has a version of carbonara, and this is mine. The chili is a nod to my favourite city, Rome, where cooks always add a little hot *peperoncini* (or sexy tickle as I like to think of it) to pasta dishes, but it also slows me down from inhaling large portions of this for supper. This is a comforting dish that's also nourishing in an old-fashioned way—my mom used to make me eat a plate of carbonara before I headed into a sixteen-hour restaurant shift. The bacon was important, she insisted. I never argued!

I only use part of an egg when it's absolutely necessary, and this is one of those times. Otherwise the sauce won't cling to the pasta. Add the whites to tomorrow's omelette or scrambled eggs. Serve this with Lemony Broiled Asparagus (page 182) or Roasted Broccoli with Lemon and Parmesan (page 188).

....

1. Boil linguine in a large pot of well-salted water until just tender, about 9 minutes or according to package directions.

2. Meanwhile, cook the bacon in a medium frying pan over medium heat until crispy. Add the chili flakes (if using) and cook another 30 seconds, then drain the bacon on paper towels, reserving the fat in the pan. Coarsely chop the bacon.

3. Whisk the egg yolks and cream together in a large serving bowl. Whisk in 1 to 2 tablespoons of the reserved bacon fat (with the chili flakes). Whisk in the Parmesan and salt. Season generously with pepper.

4. As soon as the pasta is ready, use tongs to transfer it directly into the serving bowl and toss it enthusiastically so the egg mixture coats every strand.

5. Divide between 2 or 3 warmed bowls (see Tip on page 157) and sprinkle with bacon and additional Parmesan. Serve immediately.

Tip Measuring portions of pasta is effortless with a scale. A standard portion of dry pasta is 3 ounces (85 g), while a very hungry person or teenager usually wants 4 ounces (115 g).

Chilled Cucumber and Sesame Noodles with Tofu

Serves 4 • Make ahead

This is one of my favourite summer dishes. The cucumber is refreshing, and the edamame and tofu add heft without making the dish heavy. Many pasta salads end up tasting bland, but the sesame dressing here is robust and flavourful, and a welcome, cool supper for hot days. This is also a great dish to serve at a party or potluck, since it can be both a good side dish and a delicious one-dish meal for vegetarians and vegans. I love frozen shelled edamame and always keep a bag in the freezer.

....

1. Boil spaghettini in a large pot of salted water until just tender, about 9 minutes or according to package directions. Drain and rinse with cold water until completely cool. This not only cools the noodles but also prevents them from sticking to each other.

2. Meanwhile, to make the Sesame Dressing, whisk the soy sauce, white wine vinegar, tahini, maple syrup, sesame oil and water in a large bowl. Add the tofu, cucumber, edamame and cooled spaghettini and toss gently but well.

3. Divide among 4 bowls. Garnish with green onions.

Make ahead The dressing keeps well in the fridge for up to 4 days. The salad keeps well for up to 4 hours in the fridge. Stir well before serving.

Switch it up Skip the tofu and serve this alongside barbecued chicken or steak.

Prep Time 15 minutes
Ready In about 20 minutes

9 ounces (250 g) spaghettini or soba noodles

Sesame Dressing

5 teaspoons soy sauce

1 tablespoon white wine vinegar

1 tablespoon tahini

2 teaspoons pure maple syrup

2 teaspoons sesame oil

¼ cup cold water

1 pound (450 g) firm tofu, cut into sticks

1 large seedless cucumber, sliced into thin half-moons

1 cup frozen shelled edamame, thawed

2 green onions, thinly sliced, for garnish

Uncomplicated Tomato Sauce

Makes 5 cups • Make ahead • Batch cooking

Prep Time 5 minutes or less
Ready In a little over 1 hour

2 cans (28 ounces/796 mL each) whole tomatoes

1 yellow onion, peeled and cut into quarters

2 cloves garlic, smashed

¼ cup extra-virgin olive oil or butter

¼ teaspoon salt

Although this recipe is as simple as can be, it's wonderfully versatile and the flavour is extraordinary. Why bother chopping and sautéing onions and garlic when you can simply simmer them with tomatoes? And there you have the heart of this book: food doesn't have to be complicated to be good—in fact, the opposite is usually true. This sauce is perfect with Italian Meatballs with Lemon and Parsley (page 99), Ravioli Lasagna (page 165) or Ricotta Dumplings (page 136), or use it as the sauce on Vegetable Pizza (page 132). It also makes a fantastic gift for new parents, new homeowners or students—anyone who could use a tasty home-cooked meal in a hurry. Package it in a mason jar, then bundle together with some good-quality dry pasta.

....

1. Combine tomatoes and their juices, onion and garlic in a medium saucepan. Bring to a boil. Reduce heat and simmer gently—uncovered, stirring every now and then and breaking up the tomatoes and onions a little—for 1 hour to 1 hour and 15 minutes or until the onions are very soft.

2. Add olive oil and salt and purée with an immersion blender or in a regular blender.

Make ahead Cool the sauce, then freeze it in 1-cup portions for up to 3 months.

Batch cooking Double the recipe. Cool the sauce, then freeze it in 1-cup portions for up to 3 months.

Ravioli Lasagna

Serves 6

I adore lasagna, but not the time and effort it takes to make. This recipe is a happy alternative. Adding a layer of spinach and ricotta makes it more than just baked ravioli, and it comes together in a flash, so it's ideal for weeknights. I prefer cheese ravioli for this, but you can use whatever you like best. Serve with a big green salad and crusty bread, or even Superfood Chicken Caesar Salad (page 62)—but skip the chicken.

....

1. Preheat the oven to 350°F. Spray a 9- x 13-inch baking dish (or other 12- to 14-cup baking dish) with non-stick cooking spray.

2. Combine the ravioli with 2 cups of the Uncomplicated Tomato Sauce in a large bowl. Transfer half of this ravioli mixture to the prepared baking dish and smooth into an even layer. Sprinkle evenly with the spinach, then dollop the ricotta over the top and smooth into an even layer. Sprinkle with the salt. Top with the remaining ravioli mixture.

3. Pour the remaining 1 cup Uncomplicated Tomato Sauce evenly over the top and try to tuck all the ravioli and spinach leaves under the sauce. Sprinkle with mozzarella.

4. Cover with foil and bake 20 minutes. Take off the foil, sprinkle evenly with Parmesan and bake, uncovered, another 25 to 30 minutes or until lightly golden and bubbly at the edges. Let stand 5 minutes before serving.

Tip Use fresh, refrigerated ravioli for this dish. Frozen ravioli don't cook evenly unless they are boiled.

Prep Time 10 minutes
Ready In a little over 1 hour

21 ounces (600 g) fresh cheese-and-spinach ravioli

3 cups Uncomplicated Tomato Sauce (page 162) or store-bought marinara sauce, divided

3 cups tightly packed baby spinach

2 cups ricotta cheese (about 15 ounces/425 g)

¼ teaspoon salt

1½ cups shredded mozzarella cheese

¾ cup freshly grated Parmesan cheese

One-Pot Pasta Alfredo

Serves 2 to 3

Prep Time 5 minutes
Ready In about 20 minutes

8 ounces (225 g) gemelli or penne

1 clove garlic, peeled and poked several times with a fork

¼ cup butter

½ cup whipping (35%) cream

1 cup finely grated Parmesan cheese, divided

⅛ teaspoon salt

Freshly grated nutmeg (optional)

Fresh black pepper

Pasta Alfredo is luxury on a plate. It works perfectly next to roast chicken for a fancy dinner party, and it's comfort exemplified on its own, eaten straight out of the pot after a bad day. I didn't grow up with Alfredo sauce but was introduced to it while working in a terrific gourmet shop in Nova Scotia. We made vats of sauce and sold it in 1-cup containers to be taken home. I always tried to find a crust of bread so I could scrape out the dregs of the sauce from the pot.

This trick using the garlic clove to stir the sauce is an oldie but a goodie. It adds depth of flavour without making the sauce garlicky. It's critical to use 35% whipping cream here; otherwise the sauce will split.

I like to serve this with a simple vegetable like Lemony Broiled Asparagus (page 182), Roasted Broccoli with Lemon and Parmesan (page 188) or Celery and Fennel Salad (page 178).

....

1. Boil gemelli in a large pot of well-salted water until almost tender, about 9 minutes or 1 minute less than package directions (the pasta will keep cooking in the sauce). Drain the pasta and immediately put the empty pot back on the stove over medium heat.

2. Spear the poked garlic securely onto a fork and rub it all around the inside of the pot. (Set aside, keeping the garlic on the fork.) Add the butter. Once it melts, add the cream, stirring with the fork-speared garlic as vigorously as you like—the more you stir, the more garlicky the flavour. After about 1 minute, add ¾ cup of the Parmesan and the salt, and stir until the sauce starts to simmer.

3. Add the pasta and nutmeg (if using) and cook, stirring well, about 30 seconds or until the sauce coats the pasta well. Serve with the remaining ¼ cup Parmesan and lots of pepper.

Tip Freshly grated nutmeg is a world apart from the dried powder. The next time you pass a bulk food store, pick up a couple (they look like little brown balls). They keep for several years. Grate as needed on a microplane.

Pasta Puttanesca

Serves 2 to 3

Food writers tend to dwell on this sauce's name, which references the Italian word for prostitute, but I think the way the dish materializes out of an almost-empty kitchen is far more interesting. Jars of capers, olives and anchovies keep for at least three months in the fridge, as do tins of tomatoes and dry pasta in the pantry, making this the ultimate lazy supper. Walk into the kitchen, put a pot of water on to boil and start adding ingredients to a pan. Dinner will be ready before you know it.

Even if you don't like anchovies, please trust me and try one here. I promise that it disappears into the sauce, leaving behind no fishy flavour but only a rich saltiness that makes this sauce addictive. Serve with a side of Lemony Broiled Asparagus (page 182) or a simple green salad.

....

1. Boil spaghetti in a large pot of salted water until just tender, about 9 minutes or according to package directions.

2. Meanwhile, heat the olive oil in a large frying pan over medium-low heat. Add the garlic and cook 2 to 3 minutes or until it starts to sizzle a little bit. Add the anchovy and chili flakes (if using) and cook, stirring occasionally and mashing up the anchovy, 2 to 3 minutes or until the garlic is soft. Stir in the tomatoes and bring to a simmer. Add the olives and capers and cook 2 to 4 minutes or until the sauce is hot and bubbly.

3. Use tongs to transfer the spaghetti into the sauce and stir it around so every strand is coated. Serve immediately topped with Parmesan.

Tip 1. Start by putting the water on to boil, then prep and cook the sauce. The sauce will be ready long before the pasta is ready, so just keep it warm until you're ready to add the spaghetti. 2. For this dish, don't use the liquidy diced tomatoes in a large can (28 ounce/796 mL). You need the thick and saucy ones that come in a smaller tin, often with a flip-top lid. Aurora and Mutti both make excellent versions.

Prep Time 10 minutes or less
Ready In about 20 minutes

8 ounces (225 g) spaghetti

3 tablespoons extra-virgin olive oil

2 cloves garlic, thinly sliced

1 to 2 anchovy fillets

¼ teaspoon hot chili flakes (optional)

1 can (14 ounces/398 mL) diced tomatoes (see Tip)

½ cup Kalamata olives, pitted and chopped

1 tablespoon drained capers, chopped

Freshly grated Parmesan cheese

Garlic Spaghetti

Serves 2

Prep Time 5 minutes
Ready In less than 20 minutes

8 ounces (225 g) spaghetti
or other pasta

2 tablespoons butter

1 tablespoon canola oil

2 cloves garlic, thinly sliced

½ teaspoon hot chili flakes
(optional)

Extra-virgin olive oil

Freshly grated Parmesan
cheese, for serving

This is one of the recipes that inspired this book. When people tell me they never have time to cook, I sometimes ask—in my saucier moods, anyway—if they don't even have time for garlic spaghetti. The usual response is that making pasta isn't cooking. Well, it is in my books! Sure, this dish is simple, but it's also extremely delicious. I've lost track of the number of times in my life I've been so close to ordering delivery only to realize that garlic spaghetti is faster, cheaper and smarter.

So put down the phone—you do not need a pizza. Even if your pantry is truly bare, I bet there's still half a box of pasta and a few cloves of garlic around, right? (Yes, even that dried-out clump of tiny garlic cloves that has been around for weeks counts.) Put on a pot of water. Dinner is 20 minutes away.

1. Boil spaghetti in a large pot of well-salted water until just tender, about 9 minutes or according to package directions.

2. Meanwhile, heat the butter and canola oil in a medium frying pan over low heat. Add the garlic and chili flakes, if using—they should barely sizzle. The idea is to cook them gently so they flavour the butter without getting even the slightest bit golden. Cook, stirring once in a while, 3 to 4 minutes or until the garlic is translucent.

3. As soon as the pasta is ready, use tongs to transfer it directly into the garlic pan and toss so the butter mixture coats every strand.

4. Divide between 2 warmed bowls (see Tip on page 157) and drizzle with a little olive oil. Serve with Parmesan.

Tip Cooking garlic in a mixture of butter and canola oil prevents it from singeing.

Switch it up Cook some chopped bacon in the pan first before lowering the heat and adding garlic. You can also add a handful of frozen peas to the pasta water about 1 minute before pasta is cooked.

Chili-Garlic Rapini Pasta

Serves 4 • Make ahead

Rapini, a green vegetable that looks like a cross between broccoli and chard, is mostly misunderstood. It's sturdy and naturally bitter, and it needs to be cooked slowly in lots of liquid (unlike broccoli and chard) so it becomes tender and mellow. It still retains an edge of pleasant bitterness, which, combined with olive oil, garlic and chili, is the backbone to this pasta dish.

Typically, pasta with rapini also includes sausage and Parmesan cheese—it's one of those classic Italian combinations. It's terrific, but I was thrilled to discover that this dish needs neither meat nor cheese to make it addictively tasty. The key ingredient in this recipe is salt, which brings all the flavours together. Serve this with some good bread, or even a crunchy salad such as Carrot-Lemon Slaw (page 189).

Prep Time 15 minutes or less
Ready In about ½ hour

1 pound (450 g) orecchiette or farfalle

1 bunch rapini (about 1 pound/ 450 g)

2 tablespoons extra-virgin olive oil, plus more for serving

5 cloves garlic, minced

½ teaspoon hot chili flakes

½ teaspoon salt

½ cup water

1. Boil pasta in a large pot of well-salted water until just tender, about 11 minutes or according to package directions.

2. Meanwhile, trim off and discard the tough stems of the rapini, then chop the rapini into about 1-inch lengths (you should have 6 cups, packed).

3. Heat the olive oil in a large frying pan over medium-low. Add the garlic and chili flakes and cook 1 minute or until just sizzling. Add the rapini, salt and water. Cover, reduce heat to low and simmer gently 10 minutes or until the rapini is very tender. Uncover and cook another 2 minutes or so. There should still be some liquid in the pan and the rapini should be very tender and saucy.

4. Once the pasta is cooked, drain, transfer to the frying pan and stir well. Divide among 4 warmed bowls (see Tip on page 157). Drizzle with olive oil.

Make ahead Cook the rapini up to 1 day in advance. Reheat gently before adding pasta and tossing well.

Three-Ingredient Mac and Cheese

Serves 3

Prep Time 10 minutes or less
Ready In about 20 minutes

½ pound (225 g, or half a box) elbow macaroni, fusilli or other short pasta

1 cup whipping (35%) cream

2 cups grated old Cheddar cheese

Like most children, I adored Kraft Dinner. When we lived in Nepal in the 1980s, visitors from home would bring me a box or two, which I clung to like a life raft. After we moved back to Canada, I ate it as often as I could. Even when my palate eventually wanted a slightly less chemical taste, I never wanted to give up the speed and convenience of good old KD. Was there a way to get my mac and cheese hit without going through the whole process of making a separate cheese sauce?

You betcha. And just like KD, you only need one pot. This is fast, simple and profoundly tasty. It's also easy to scale down: when Thomas was young I made it in small portions, and quickly made more when the tiny dictator decided he liked it. You can use any kind of Cheddar—orange for little ones with tender palates, or best-quality aged stuff. Serve with a green salad.

....

1. Boil macaroni in a large pot of well-salted water until almost tender, about 10 minutes or 1 minute less than package directions (pasta will keep cooking in the sauce). Drain.

2. While the pasta drains, put the pot back on low heat. Add the cream, then the cheese. Stir, increasing the heat as you need to in order to speed things along, until the cheese melts into a sauce.

3. Add the pasta to the sauce and stir enthusiastically for 1 to 2 minutes or until the sauce thickens and clings to each noodle. Serve right away.

Tip 1. For a fancy upgrade, top it off with fresh black pepper and chopped fresh chives, tarragon, parsley or all three. **2.** It's essential to salt pasta cooking water generously. This is the only chance you'll get to boost the flavour of the actual noodles, so it's even more important when the sauce is simple (as it is here and in most of my pasta recipes). For every 2 L (quarts) of water, add 1 teaspoon of salt. My students are often surprised when they see me do this, but once they taste the finished dish, they find it all makes sense.

Five-Minute Vegetable Sides

Minty Peas

Serves 4

Prep Time 5 minutes or less
Ready In about 10 minutes

2 cups frozen peas

2 tablespoons butter

⅛ teaspoon salt

2 tablespoons mint sauce

¼ cup chopped fresh mint (optional)

Mint and peas are a match made in heaven, but since I don't always have the fresh stuff, I usually use bottled mint sauce, which keeps almost endlessly in the fridge. It's important to use runny mint sauce, not the congealed (usually lurid green) mint jelly. This is a perfect match for Lemony Lamb Chops (page 109), but it's also great with Herb and Garlic Meatloaf (page 91) or Weekday Roast Chicken (page 65).

....

1. Drop the peas into a medium pot of boiling salted water. Boil 2 minutes. Drain, then immediately put the empty pot back on the stove over medium heat.

2. Add the butter and stir to melt. Add the peas and salt and stir to coat. Remove from the heat and stir in mint sauce and fresh mint, if using. Serve immediately.

Celery and Fennel Salad

Serves 4

Prep Time 5 minutes
Ready In about 10 minutes

½ fennel bulb, trimmed

2 stalks celery

2 tablespoons fresh lemon juice

⅛ teaspoon salt

2 tablespoons extra-virgin olive oil

2 tablespoons chopped fresh cilantro or parsley

Fresh black pepper

This is a marriage of two perpetually forgotten veggies—celery and fennel. They amplify each other, and although both are winter vegetables, they're crispy and refreshing any time of year. Add a ball of best-quality fresh mozzarella torn into pieces and call this lunch. This is great any time you need a fresh, crunchy side dish, such as when serving Herb and Garlic Meatloaf (page 91) or Ravioli Lasagna (page 165).

....

1. Thinly slice the fennel crosswise, discarding the core. Thinly slice the celery on a bit of an angle to get longer pieces. Toss the vegetables with lemon juice and salt and let stand 5 minutes.

2. Stir in the olive oil and cilantro. Season well with pepper and serve.

Sweet-and-Sour Bok Choy

Serves 4

Lots of greenhouses now grow different types of baby-sized Asian greens like bok choy, and they are available year-round. This easy, rich sauce goes well with any type of Asian greens. The sauciness of this recipe makes it a great fit with Baked Lemon Salmon (page 112), Teriyaki Chicken Skewers (page 75) or Soy-Ginger Tofu (page 139).

....

1. Stir the sugar with soy sauce, rice wine vinegar and chili-garlic sauce (if using) in a small bowl until the sugar dissolves. Stir in the cornstarch. Reserve.

2. Place the bok choy in a frying pan that's wide enough to fit the bulbs all in a single layer. Add the water, cover and bring to a boil. Cook 3 minutes or until the stems are tender-crisp when poked with a sharp knife. Take off the lid and cook, shaking the pan a few times, until the pan is dry, about 1 minute.

3. Stir the soy sauce mixture and add it to the pan. Cook, stirring constantly, 10 to 30 seconds or until the sauce thickens and coats the bok choy. Serve immediately.

Prep Time 5 minutes
Ready In about 10 minutes

1 tablespoon granulated sugar

1 tablespoon soy sauce

1 tablespoon rice wine vinegar

½ teaspoon hot chili-garlic sauce (optional)

1 teaspoon cornstarch

1 pound (450 g) baby bok choy, washed well

¼ cup water

Lemony Broiled Asparagus

Serves 4

Prep Time 5 minutes
Ready In about 10 minutes

1 large bunch asparagus
(about 16 spears)

1 tablespoon canola oil

⅛ teaspoon salt

1 lemon

Fresh black pepper

I prefer medium to fat asparagus spears, which are sweeter and juicier than the pencil-thin ones, but if they are quite fat, use a vegetable peeler to remove the thick skin from the lower half of each spear. This pairs well with many dishes, including Italian Roast Pork (page 216), Garlic Spaghetti (page 170) and Easy Cheddar Soufflé (page 144).

1. Position an oven rack about 6 inches below the broiler and preheat the broiler. Line a large rimmed baking sheet with foil.

2. Snap off and discard the thick, tough bottom portion of the asparagus spears, then place them on the baking sheet. Drizzle with the canola oil, then toss asparagus well to coat. Spread out in a single layer. Sprinkle with salt.

3. Broil, shaking the pan once to move the spears around a bit, 4 to 7 minutes or until the asparagus is lightly browned and tender-crisp.

4. Zest the lemon right over top. Season with pepper. Serve immediately.

Cabbage with Vinaigrette

Serves 4

Most of the world runs away in horror at the mere suggestion of boiled cabbage. I beg you to reconsider. Cooked this way, it is tender-crisp and not mushy at all, and slathered in tangy vinaigrette it's a delightful surprise. Use firm green cabbage (not crinkly, tender Savoy). I often serve this alongside Weekday Roast Chicken (page 65) or Rosemary-Roasted Pork Tenderloin (page 103).

....

1. Bring a large pot of salted water to a boil. Combine the lemon juice, mustard, honey and salt in a mason jar and shake well. Add the olive oil and shake until emulsified.

2. Add the cabbage to the boiling water. As soon as the water returns to a rolling boil, drain the cabbage. Transfer it to a large bowl and drizzle it with the vinaigrette. Season with pepper. Serve immediately.

Prep Time about 5 minutes
Ready In about 15 minutes

2 tablespoons fresh lemon juice

1 tablespoon Dijon mustard

1 teaspoon liquid honey

½ teaspoon salt

¼ cup extra-virgin olive oil

½ green cabbage, cored and cut into thin wedges

Fresh black pepper

Jacket Potatoes

Serves 4

Prep Time less than 5 minutes
Ready In about 1 hour

4 large evenly shaped and
sized Yukon Gold potatoes

Butter

Flaky sea salt

Fresh black pepper

Potatoes "in their jackets" sound like adorable characters from a children's book, but it's just a better name for versatile and delicious baked spuds. I have to include the recipe because every time I make these for company (which is often—they go with almost everything and require zero effort) my guests are both dazzled and full of questions about the technique. These truly do go with everything, but especially Fresh Vegetable Chili (page 140), Pan-Seared Rib-Eye Steak (page 88), Lemony Lamb Chops (page 109) and Rosemary-Roasted Pork Tenderloin (page 103).

....

1. Preheat the oven to 400°F. Scrub the potatoes and poke each one a few times with a fork. Place directly on the oven rack. Bake 50 minutes to 1 hour or until tender when pierced all the way through with a paring knife.

2. Cut an X in the top of each potato, then gently press on either side of the X to open up the potato a little. Serve with butter, flaky sea salt and fresh black pepper.

Grilled Corn

Serves 4

I used to think grilling corn was complicated, and required pre-soaking so it wouldn't burn. Then a visiting chef friend simply chucked a dozen ears on the barbecue and walked away. The results were fantastic, and it couldn't be easier! Add to a meal of Maple-Garlic Cedar Salmon (page 232), Soy and Garlic Grilled Flank Steak (page 95) or Slow-Cooker Sweet and Spicy Ribs (page 106).

Prep Time less than 5 minutes
Ready In about 20 minutes

8 ears of corn, husks on

....

1. Preheat the grill to medium-high heat. Open the top of the husk of each ear of corn just a little at the top and yank out as much of the corn silk as you can. Replace the husk.

2. Place ears of corn directly on the grill. Grill, turning occasionally, 12 to 17 minutes or until the husks are slightly burnt on all sides and the corn is tender. To check if corn is done, peel back the husk a bit. The kernels should be glossy and dark yellow.

3. Peel and serve with butter and salt if you must, but I like this best totally naked.

Curry-Spiced Roasted Squash

Serves 4

Prep Time 5 minutes
Ready In about 30 minutes

1 acorn squash

2 tablespoons canola oil

1 teaspoon curry powder

¼ teaspoon salt

The sweetness of squash matches perfectly with curry. Since it's nearly impossible to peel acorn squash, just wash it well and eat the skin. This side is a bit of a chameleon, so serve it with anything from Dry-Brined Turkey (page 213) to Slow-Cooker Sweet and Spicy Ribs (page 106) or Herb and Garlic Meatloaf (page 91).

....

1. Preheat the oven to 375°F. Line a rimmed baking sheet with foil.

2. Scrub the squash well, then cut it in half and scoop out and discard the seeds. Cut each half into 5 or 6 slices.

3. Place the squash slices on the prepared baking sheet and drizzle with canola oil. Toss to coat with the oil. Mix the curry powder and salt together and sprinkle all over the squash. Bake 20 to 25 minutes or until tender.

Roasted Broccoli with Lemon and Parmesan

Serves 4

Prep Time 5 minutes
Ready In about 20 minutes

1 large bunch broccoli

2 tablespoons canola oil

¼ teaspoon salt

1 lemon

Freshly grated Parmesan cheese (optional)

I'm crazy about roasted broccoli. The high heat turns parts of the florets into crunchy little flavour bombs without turning the rest of the broccoli to mush. Try this alongside Lemon and Herb Salmon Loaf (page 119), Easy Cheddar Soufflé (page 144) or Easier Chicken and Parmesan Risotto (page 71).

....

1. Preheat the oven to 425°F. Line a large rimmed baking sheet with foil or parchment paper.

2. Cut broccoli into large florets. Peel the stems and cut into big chunks. Transfer to the prepared baking sheet. Drizzle with canola oil and toss well to coat. Spread out in a single layer. Sprinkle with salt.

3. Roast 15 to 20 minutes or until parts of the broccoli are golden and crispy.

4. Zest the lemon right over top so the broccoli catches all the fragrant oil. Sprinkle with Parmesan, if using. Serve immediately.

Carrot-Lemon Slaw

Serves 4 • Make ahead

The genius in this dish is the lemon and salt marinade. It draws out the natural sweetness of the carrots and creates a dressing. The spices and raisins give the dish a Moroccan flavour, but it's equally delicious without them. This easygoing side dish pairs well with anything from Teriyaki Chicken Skewers (page 75) to Secret-Ingredient Chicken Burgers with Cilantro Salsa (page 80) to Lemony Lamb Chops (page 109).

....

1. Peel and grate the carrots. Place them in a serving bowl, then stir in the lemon juice and salt. Let stand 10 minutes. (There should be lots of orange liquid in the bottom of the bowl.)

2. Add the olive oil, parsley, and raisins and cumin (if using) and stir well. Serve right away or store in the fridge for up to 24 hours.

Make ahead This keeps well in the fridge for up to 24 hours.

Switch it up Replace some of the carrots with grated unpeeled apples, cabbage or raw beets. Add crumbled feta and chopped toasted almonds.

Prep Time 5 minutes or less
Ready In about 15 minutes

6 medium carrots

¼ cup fresh lemon juice

½ teaspoon salt

3 tablespoons extra-virgin olive oil

¼ cup chopped fresh parsley

¼ cup raisins or currants (optional)

¼ teaspoon ground cumin or cinnamon, or both (optional)

Uncomplicated Entertaining

UNCOMPLICATED DINNER PARTIES AND MENUS

How to Host an Uncomplicated Dinner Party

I love hosting dinner parties. In fact, I think it's officially my hobby—more than knitting or skiing—since I do it so often and it brings me so much joy. With that in mind, I'm always determined to be as relaxed as possible, not only when the guests arrive but also during the prep time, and that takes some strategy. Here are the rules I set for myself:

1. Just do it! Don't worry about making fancy food, polishing the silver or inviting everyone you know. Just invite people you enjoy being with, people you know will make for a fun evening. Pick a menu and go for it, remembering that the party is about spending time with people you like, not blowing them away with your take on chicken liver pâté. (Being a food professional, I have to remind myself of this fairly often.)

2. Plan a menu for the time and the kitchen you have. It's way better to calmly serve pasta and salad than to get yourself into a tizzy trying to serve roast dinner with all the trimmings. Make sure everything that needs the oven can be cooked at the same temperature (unless you're lucky enough to have two ovens, of course).

3. Do as much in advance as you possibly can. Do all the shopping, make the dessert, prep the vegetables, and even assemble or cook the main course at least a day before. I aim to have only one or two dishes left to finish off at dinner time. This means often serving one side dish hot and one deliberately at room temperature.

4. Never serve a first course. There is simply no way for you to sit down and enjoy a first course, like soup, while simultaneously putting the finishing touches on the main course.

5. Stand-up parties are fun for big groups—just make sure to serve things that can be eaten easily with one hand. But do consider a sit-down party for an intimate gathering, as they feel more special and allow for better conversations! I often throw a tablecloth over my dining table and an extra folding table to create one huge table. Add seating with a piano bench, office chairs or even bar stools. It's really fun.

6. Don't worry about stocking the bar with every liquor in the shop. If you and your pals enjoy a cocktail, make up a pitcher of one type in advance (see pages 196 to 203) and have red and white wine available. It's also a nice idea to have a couple of different beers on hand. Don't forget something interesting for those who don't drink.

7. Guests will usually ask, "What can I bring?" I almost always answer, "Nothing except your appetite," because I want my guests to feel totally relaxed. There is one exception: when one of the guests is an enthusiastic cook who is going to show up with something homemade regardless of what you say, you can certainly suggest a dessert, a salad, a pre-mixed cocktail or an appetizer (unless that person is perpetually late to parties).

8. I feel pretty strongly that you need to round out the meal with a little something sweet at the end. If you're like me and love to bake, have at it. But remember that good ice cream, fancy cookies or chocolates are also perfectly acceptable.

9. Only use your good dishes and glassware if you'll have time the morning after to wash them by hand. Otherwise, use the dishwasher-safe stuff, and empty the dishwasher before the party starts so you can load it before bedtime.

10. If dinner parties aren't fun for you, don't host them. It's as simple as that. Parties should be a delight, not a chore. The secret to a memorable party is easy: good company served good food that doesn't require you to be in the kitchen, missing out on the best moments.

Menus for Entertaining

If there is a make-ahead tip in the recipe, use it! Also, make double batches if the guest lists require. Round out these menus with green salads and/or good bread.

World's Easiest Dinner Party (for 4)
Weekday Roast Chicken (page 65)
Supper Salad (page 47)

Friday After-Work Party (for 4)
Mojitos (page 200)
Pasta Puttanesca (page 169)
Grown-Up Ice Cream Sundaes (page 272)

Summer Barbecue (for 6)
Fresh Tomato and Corn Salsa (page 209)
Soy and Garlic Grilled Flank Steak (page 95)
Greek Orzo Salad with Basil (page 223)
Raspberry Shortcakes (page 245)

Dinner with In-laws (for 4)
Broiled Miso Salmon (page 116)
Lemony Broiled Asparagus (page 182)
Lemon Custards (page 263)

Make-Ahead Dinner with Friends (for 6)
Sailor's Rum Punch (page 197)
British-Style Fish Pie (page 115)
One-Pot Chocolate-Pecan Brownies (page 267)

Summer Family Birthday (for 8)
Lemon and Spice Grilled Chicken (page 79)
Grilled Chili-Lime Shrimp (page 123)
French Potato Salad (page 220)
No-Bake Coconut Cream Cake (page 246)

Winter Family Birthday (for 8)
Sweet and Spicy Popcorn (page 205)
Saucy Pot Roast (page 96)
Chocolate Fudge Layer Cake (page 237)

Weeknight Vegetarian Dinner Party (for 6)
Ravioli Lasagna (page 165)
Apple Crisp (page 259)

Autumn Vegetarian Dinner Party (for 6)
Mushroom and Thyme Pâté (page 208)
Ricotta Dumplings (page 136)
Supper Salad (page 47)
Plum-Almond Galette (page 255)

Gluten-Free Dinner (for 4)
Sweet and Spicy Popcorn (page 205)
Chicken with Garlic and Prunes (page 228)
Lemon Custards (page 263)

New Year's Eve Party (for 8)
Gin Martinis (page 203)
Warm Dates with Orange Zest and Olive Oil (page 209)
Italian Roast Pork (page 216)
Balsamic Roasted Vegetables (page 219)
Chocolate Silk Pie (page 252)

Make-Ahead Holiday Feast (for 12)
Mulled Wine (page 196)
Spiced Party Nuts (page 210)
Dry-Brined Turkey (page 213)
Make-Ahead Scalloped Potatoes (page 227)
Balsamic Roasted Vegetables (page 219)
Celery and Fennel Salad (page 178)
Gingerbread Bundt Cake with Lemon Glaze (page 238)

Neighbourhood Drop-In Party (for 25 or more)
Mulled Wine (page 196)
Spiced Party Nuts (page 210)
Easy Maple-Mustard Ham (page 224)
Fresh Vegetable Chili (page 140)
Buns, mustards, chutneys
Date-Coconut Squares (page 264)

Mulled Wine

Serves 10

1 orange

1½ cups sweet apple cider (non-alcoholic)

3 tablespoons granulated sugar (optional)

1 tablespoon whole cloves

3 cinnamon sticks

2 star anise (optional)

2 bottles (26 ounces/750 mL each) dry red wine

One memorable Halloween night, our neighbours handed out candy to the kids and cups of warm spiced wine to the chaperones. On a chilly fall evening, there couldn't have been anything better. This is also great for a holiday drop-in party.

....

1. Use a vegetable peeler to take the zest off the orange in long strips. Drop the zest into a medium pot, then juice the orange and add the juice to the pot as well. Add the apple cider, sugar (if using) and spices. Bring to a boil, then reduce heat and simmer 5 minutes.

2. Add the red wine and heat gently (but do not boil) until heated through. Serve warm.

Rosé Sangria

Serves 5

1 bottle (26 ounces/750 mL) dry rosé wine

1 cup white grape juice

⅓ cup fresh lemon juice

2 ounces Triple Sec or Cointreau

3 cups raspberries, melon balls or peeled peach slices (or a mix)

Lighter and prettier than red sangria, this punch is perfect for a grown-up tea party.

....

1. Mix ingredients together in a large pitcher. Chill at least 4 hours.

Sailor's Rum Punch

Serves 8

Punch has a long and interesting history, and the original (as far as I can tell) is more of a formula than an exact recipe. The saying is "1 of sour, 2 of sweet, 3 of strong and 4 of weak," meaning one measure of something sour like citrus juice; double that quantity of sweet syrup (or grenadine); triple it to measure the strong, or alcohol; then tone it all down with four times the original measure of a weak ingredient like water, or tea, which adds a lovely bit of bitterness and a deeper colour. I like to serve this as the welcome cocktail at outdoor parties that start in the afternoon.

½ cup fresh lime or lemon juice

1 cup Simple Syrup (recipe below)

12 ounces dark rum

2 cups brewed black tea, caffeinated or decaffeinated

1. Stir lime juice, Simple Syrup, rum and tea with ice, then strain into rocks glasses filled with ice.

Simple Syrup

1. Combine 1 cup granulated sugar with 1 cup water in a small pot. Bring to a boil, stirring to dissolve the sugar. Chill, then store in the fridge for up to 2 months.

Mojitos

Serves 4

20 fresh mint leaves, plus 4 sprigs of mint

⅓ cup Simple Syrup (page 197)

8 ounces white rum

½ cup fresh lime juice

2 to 6 dashes orange bitters (optional)

1 lime, cut into rounds, for garnish

These pretty drinks originating in Cuba make a bright and cheerful start to a summer dinner party. Fresh mint is crucial, and it's best when it's just pulled from the garden.

....

1. Muddle or bash the mint leaves and Simple Syrup together in a large measuring cup. Stir in the rum, lime juice and bitters, if using.

2. Fill 4 glasses three-quarters of the way with ice cubes, then tuck the mint springs in and around the ice. Add the rum mixture. Garnish with lime.

White Michelada

Serves 2

I first tasted something like this on a hot summer night at a taco restaurant in Toronto, and it knocked my socks off. It's refreshing and bursting with flavour. But don't be fooled that it's sweet and bubbly and goes down easily— it's still a serious drink.

Spicy Lime Sugar-Salt
(recipe below; optional)

6 tablespoons fresh lime juice

¼ cup Simple Syrup
(page 197)

2 ounces tequila

1 bottle Mexican beer,
such as Corona, chilled

....

1. Prepare 2 tall glasses with Spicy Lime Sugar-Salt, if using. Fill with ice.

2. Combine lime juice, Simple Syrup and tequila in a shaker filled with ice. Shake well. Strain into prepared glasses and top with beer.

Spicy Lime Sugar-Salt

1. Combine 2 tablespoons granulated sugar with the zest of 1 lime, ½ teaspoon kosher salt and a pinch of cayenne. Rub a cut lime around the rim of a glass, then dip into sugar-salt to create a crusted rim.

Bombay Banker

Serves 2

4 ounces rye

1½ ounces Chai-Infused Red Vermouth (recipe below)

2 to 6 dashes Angostura bitters

Candied ginger, for garnish

A classic Manhattan is one of my favourite cocktails, but when I was developing recipes for my cocktails class I stumbled on an inspired flavour match in chai-spiced red vermouth. It makes a Manhattan exotic and very special, and my students always fall in love with it. For the classic, just use plain red vermouth.

1. Combine the rye, Chai-Infused Red Vermouth and bitters in a shaker filled with ice. Shake or stir, then strain into a martini glass. Garnish with a piece of candied ginger.

Chai-Infused Red Vermouth

1. Combine 1 cup red vermouth with 1 chai tea bag in a mason jar. Cover and steep at room temperature for 24 hours. Remove the tea bag and keep the vermouth refrigerated for up to 2 months.

Gin Martini

Serves 2

Hands-down, a gin martini is my favourite drink on earth, and how I unwind almost every Friday night. It's bracing and refreshing, just as every great cocktail should be. Plymouth is my dream gin, but trying this recipe with new gins is part of the fun.

5 ounces Plymouth gin

1½ ounces dry white vermouth

1 to 3 dashes orange bitters

Lemon twist, for garnish

1. Combine the gin, white vermouth and bitters in a shaker filled with ice. Stir well, quickly, then immediately strain into 2 martini glasses. Garnish with a lemon twist.

Tip For best results, store the gin in the freezer and the vermouth in the fridge.

Cucumber Fridge Pickles

Serves 4 • Make ahead

Prep Time 15 minutes
Ready In about 7 hours

2½ cups thickly sliced mini cucumbers

1 tablespoon kosher salt

1½ cups white vinegar

1 cup granulated sugar

1 teaspoon fennel or coriander seeds, slightly crushed (optional)

These crunchy sour-sweet pickles are just the right snack on a hot day. Serve them with beer and potato chips before a casual barbecue.

....

1. Combine the cucumbers and salt in a colander. Toss well, then let stand 10 minutes.

2. Combine the vinegar, sugar and fennel seeds (if using) in a small pot. Bring to a boil and cook 1 minute or until the sugar dissolves completely.

3. Rinse cucumbers well under running water, then divide between two 500 mL jars. Divide the hot vinegar mixture between the jars.

4. Let cool to room temperature, then refrigerate for at least 6 hours before serving.

Make ahead These pickles last well in the fridge for up to 5 days. They will become a little less crunchy and a little tangier as the days progress.

Sweet and Spicy Popcorn

Serves 4

Popcorn is a perfect party snack: the kernels keep for years in the pantry, it takes no time to prepare, and it has the right salty crunch to make it a good pairing with any alcohol. More often than not, it's what I serve to guests as they arrive.

This version is a quick and easy candy-corn, but the cayenne, lime and salt balance out the sweet to make it just right for serving with drinks.

Prep Time 5 minutes
Ready In about 5 minutes

½ teaspoon salt

⅛ to ¼ teaspoon cayenne

¼ cup canola oil

½ cup popcorn kernels

3 tablespoons granulated sugar

Zest of 1 lime

· ·

1. Mix the salt and cayenne together in a small dish.

2. Heat the canola oil and 3 popcorn kernels in a large, heavy pot with the lid on over medium-high heat. Once the kernels pop, add the remaining popcorn and shake the pot a bit so the kernels get coated with oil. Immediately sprinkle kernels evenly with sugar. Cover and cook, lifting and shaking the pot frequently, until the sound of popping stops, 2 to 3 minutes.

3. Remove from the heat and immediately sprinkle popcorn with the salt mixture and lime zest. Transfer to a very large bowl and stir well.

Tip Making popcorn on the stove can be a bit of an art, and I found it took me a few batches before I figured out which pot and what level of heat to use on my stove.

Mushroom and Thyme Pâté

Serves 6 • Make ahead

Prep Time 15 minutes
Ready In about 1 hour

2 packages (½ ounce/
14 g each) dried porcini
mushrooms

1 package (8 ounces/250 g)
cream cheese, at room
temperature

2 teaspoons dry sherry or
brandy

2 teaspoons fresh lemon juice

1 teaspoon packed fresh
thyme leaves (from about
7 sprigs)

¼ teaspoon salt

Dried mushrooms are little flavour supernovas. Just soak them, whirl them up with cream cheese and a few other ingredients, and you've got a delicious spread that rivals any liver pâté I've ever tasted. This is perfect for entertaining, but it also works beautifully spread on toast or slathered on a sandwich.

....

1. Boil 3 cups of water in a small pot. Add the mushrooms and let stand 10 minutes. Strain, reserving the liquid.

2. Place the soaked mushrooms in a small blender or food processor. Add the cream cheese, sherry, lemon juice, thyme, salt and 1 tablespoon of the reserved mushroom-soaking liquid (try not to take the sediment from the bottom). Purée until smooth, scraping down the sides as required.

3. Scrape into a small serving dish and smooth the top. Cover and chill at least 1 hour and as long as 2 days. Serve with sliced baguette, crostini or crackers.

Make ahead This keeps well in the fridge for up to 2 days.

Fresh Tomato and Corn Salsa

Serves 4 • Make ahead

I really don't like store-bought salsa. This recipe is so fresh-tasting and easy that you may never buy the jarred stuff again! It's terrific as a snack, served alongside tortillas and guacamole, and also as a condiment to any Tex-Mex dish, like my Saucy Tex-Mex Black Beans (page 147).

....

1. Combine tomatoes, onion, lime juice, chili (if using) and salt in a medium bowl. Let stand 5 minutes.

2. Stir in the corn and cilantro.

Make ahead This keeps well in the fridge for up to 12 hours.

Prep Time 15 minutes or less
Ready In about 15 minutes

3 medium, ripe tomatoes, finely diced

1 small yellow onion, finely chopped

¼ cup fresh lime juice

1 fresh red chili, minced (optional)

½ teaspoon salt

1 cup corn kernels (thawed if frozen)

½ cup chopped fresh cilantro

Warm Dates with Orange Zest and Olive Oil

Serves 4

Medjool dates are so luscious they don't really need dressing up, but flavouring them with orange and salt balances their sweetness, and serving them warm is a light and tasty start to a dinner party. They're also my secret-weapon snack when a guest is vegan or gluten-free.

....

1. Remove pits from the dates, while keeping the dates as whole as possible.

2. Heat the olive oil in a medium frying pan over low heat. Add the dates and cook, gently stirring from time to time, until just barely warmed through, 3 to 5 minutes. (They burn easily, so pay close attention.)

3. Transfer to a serving platter. Sprinkle with orange zest and salt.

Tip To easily remove the date pits, poke a paring knife into the centre of each date. The knife should make contact with the pit. Then just drag the knife (and pit) toward the stem end of the date and pull it out.

Prep Time 10 minutes or less
Ready In about 10 minutes

16 Medjool dates

2 tablespoons extra-virgin olive oil

Zest of 1 orange

Flaky sea salt, such as Maldon

Spiced Party Nuts

Serves 12 to 15 • Make ahead • Batch cooking

Prep Time 10 minutes or less
Ready In about 2 hours

1 egg white

¼ cup granulated sugar

1 teaspoon salt

½ teaspoon cayenne

½ teaspoon ground ginger

¼ teaspoon cinnamon

¼ teaspoon smoked paprika

3½ cups pecan or walnut halves, or a mix (about 12 ounces/350 g)

These are my favourite party snack, and they make an excellent hostess gift too. When cooked with sugar and egg white, the nuts become crunchy and stay that way for several days. The spice mixture clings best to the nooks and crannies of pecans and walnuts. Reduce the cayenne if you're serving this to children.

....

1. Preheat the oven to 300°F. Line a large rimmed baking sheet with parchment paper.

2. Whisk the egg white in a large bowl until it's foamy, then whisk in the sugar. Whisk in salt and spices until well combined. Add the nuts and stir well to coat. Transfer the nuts to the prepared baking sheet and spread out in an even layer.

3. Bake 15 minutes. Reduce heat to 250°F and bake another 10 minutes or until fragrant and just golden.

4. Let cool completely on the baking sheet. Gently separate the nuts before serving or storing.

Make ahead Store these in glass jars or resealable plastic bags at room temperature for up to 5 days.

Batch cooking Double the recipe, using 2 baking sheets and switching them around halfway through baking.

Switch it up In place of all the spices, use 1½ teaspoons curry powder.

Cheese with Chili Honey

Serves 4 to 6 • Make ahead

If you have excellent cheese, it needs nothing. This, however, is a simple way to upgrade ordinary grocery-store Brie. Leave the cheese at room temperature for at least 10 hours for maximum creaminess.

....

1. Combine honey and chili flakes in a small pot. Heat over medium-low heat until just foaming, about 3 minutes. Let cool to room temperature.

2. Place cheese on a small serving platter, then pour honey mixture over the cheese. Serve with crackers or sliced baguette.

Make ahead Prepare the chili honey and keep at room temperature for up to 1 day. Let the cheese come to room temperature (at least 6 hours). Pour honey mixture over cheese just before serving.

Prep Time 5 minutes
Ready In about 5 minutes
if the cheese is room
temperature

3 tablespoons liquid honey

½ to 1 teaspoon hot chili
flakes

1 wheel of Brie or Camembert
(7 ounces/200 g), at room
temperature

Dry-Brined Turkey

Serves 8 to 10

I've never understood exactly why brining works so well on roast turkey, but it really does make it more moist and flavourful. What I do understand, and what stays with me, is the reaction I get from guests when I serve this bird. Hands-down, it's the best turkey they've ever eaten. It's turkey magic. This roast also looks spectacular, and is always the centrepiece of my Thanksgiving table. I serve it with easy sides like Make-Ahead Scalloped Potatoes (page 227) and Balsamic Roasted Vegetables (page 219). The bones also make terrific soup.

Dry-brining is much less complicated than wet-brining since you don't need a vessel in which to submerge a turkey and keep it cold. It is absolutely critical that you use kosher salt for this, preferably Diamond Crystal. Regular salt is too fine and will permeate the fibres of the turkey, ruining everything.

....

1. Combine brown sugar with kosher salt in a medium bowl. Place the turkey in a large plastic bag (I use a grocery bag, checking first that it has no holes) and place the bag in a roasting pan.

2. Pack the sugar mixture all over the breast, legs and wings of the turkey, pressing firmly so as much of the mix sticks as possible. Carefully close up the bag, just for neatness, then pop it into the fridge (or a room that is colder than 39°F/4°C but above freezing) for 24 to 36 hours.

3. About 4 hours before you want to sit down for supper, preheat the oven to 325°F. Take the turkey out of the bag and rinse it under cold running water, gently rubbing it until every last speck of the brining mixture comes off. Don't forget to rinse out the inside, too.

4. Place the turkey on a rack in a roasting pan and dry it with paper towels. Place the thyme in the cavity and tie the legs together with twine. Bend and tuck the wing tips under the back. Brush the turkey all over with the canola oil.

5. Roast 3 to 3½ hours or until a thermometer inserted into the thickest part of the thigh reads 175°F. Transfer the turkey to a carving board and tent loosely with foil. Let rest at least 30 minutes and as much as an hour before carving.

Prep Time 20 minutes or less
Ready In about 27 hours

3 cups packed brown sugar

1½ cups kosher salt

1 fresh turkey (13 to 15 pounds/ 6 to 7 kg)

1 bunch fresh thyme, parsley or sage, or a combination

3 tablespoons canola oil

Tip 1. Resting meat of any size, but especially large roasts, is arguably the most important step. During its rest, the meat's juices will redistribute themselves and make the meat juicy and flavourful. It will also be easier to carve. The roast will cool down a little, but not enough to notice.
2. Save those bones and use them to make Slow-Cooker Chicken Stock (page 67).

Cheddar and Broccoli Gnocchi Casserole

Serves 8 to 10 • Make ahead

Prep Time 20 minutes or less
Ready In less than 1 hour

⅓ cup butter

1 yellow onion, finely chopped

⅓ cup all-purpose flour

1 teaspoon dry mustard

½ teaspoon dried thyme

¼ teaspoon cayenne (optional)

2 cups 2% milk

3 cups grated old white Cheddar cheese, divided

2.2 pounds (1 kg) plain potato gnocchi (see Tip)

1 small bunch broccoli, chopped into small pieces (about 3 cups)

Think of this as fancy mac and cheese. Oh, and easier too, since packaged gnocchi doesn't need to be cooked beforehand (unlike pasta). This is the perfect cozy comfort food dish for a casual dinner party, or for any time you'd rather not serve meat as the main course. It's also great as part of a potluck buffet, although in my experience it quickly becomes the star of the show. Serve a few crunchy vegetables sides with it, such as Carrot-Lemon Slaw (page 189) and Celery and Fennel Salad (page 178).

1. Preheat the oven to 325°F. Spray a 9- x 13-inch baking dish with non-stick cooking spray.

2. Melt the butter in a large pot over medium heat. Add the onion and cook until softened and tinged with gold, about 5 minutes. Sprinkle in the flour and stir well to incorporate. Stir in the mustard, thyme and cayenne, if using. Reduce heat to low, then add about half of the milk, stirring until the mixture is smooth and thick. Stir in the rest of the milk. Bring to a simmer and cook until just slightly thickened, about 2 minutes.

3. Add 2 cups of the cheese and stir until melted. Stir in the gnocchi and bring back to a simmer, then turn off the heat and stir in the broccoli. Transfer to the prepared baking dish.

4. Cover tightly with foil and bake 30 to 35 minutes or until bubbly at the edges. Take off the foil and sprinkle with the remaining 1 cup cheese. Broil, leaving the pan in the middle of the oven, 1 to 3 minutes or until golden. Let stand 5 minutes before serving.

Tip Use the packaged gnocchi that is sold at room temperature. It's the perfect texture for this dish (unlike refrigerated gnocchi which can get soggy). Look for it in the pasta aisle.

Make ahead Assemble the dish but do not bake. Keep refrigerated for up to 1 day. Bake as per recipe, increasing the baking time to 45 minutes.

Italian Roast Pork

Serves 8

Prep Time 15 minutes or less
Ready In about 2 hours

1 bone-in pork rib roast
(4½ to 5½ pounds/2 to 2.5 kg)

¼ teaspoon salt

2 tablespoons canola oil

¾ cup dry white wine

8 cloves garlic, peeled

4 to 8 fresh sage leaves

1 to 2 sprigs fresh rosemary

This isn't a roast in the traditional sense, but it's also not quite a braised dish, either. Instead, it's a kind of happy medium that's ideal for pork. In a closed pot in the oven, the pork becomes tender, juicy and perfumed by the wine, garlic and herbs. The sauce makes itself, and it's that deliriously tasty kind of sauce that dreams are made of. To top it all off, this dish makes the house smell so good your guests will be dazzled before they even take a bite. Serve with mashed or Jacket Potatoes (page 184) along with Lemony Broiled Asparagus (page 182) or Cabbage with Vinaigrette (page 183).

1. Preheat the oven to 325°F.

2. Dry the pork with paper towels, then sprinkle with the salt. Heat the canola oil in a large oven-safe pot or Dutch oven over medium-high heat. Add the pork and cook about 2 minutes per side or until browned all over.

3. Add the white wine, garlic, sage and rosemary. Cover and transfer to the oven. Cook about 90 minutes or until centre of pork is 160°F. Transfer pork to a platter and tent loosely with foil.

4. Place the pot over medium-high heat and bring to a boil. Boil 5 to 10 minutes, mashing the garlic as it boils, until the sauce reduces and thickens a little bit. Strain the sauce.

5. Carve the pork into thick slices and then drizzle with the sauce.

Balsamic Roasted Vegetables

Serves 8 • Make ahead

This glorious dish is another one of my secret, make-in-advance entertaining recipes. These roasted vegetables go well with any kind of main course, from Naked Burgers (page 100) to Maple-Garlic Cedar Salmon (page 232) to Dry-Brined Turkey (page 213), or even alongside a simple cheese and charcuterie board for a truly effortless supper.

....

1. Preheat the oven to 425°F. Line a large rimmed baking sheet with parchment paper.

2. Combine the onion, eggplants, peppers and zucchini on the prepared baking sheet. Drizzle with olive oil and toss well to coat. Spread into an even layer. Drizzle with balsamic vinegar and sprinkle with salt.

3. Roast, stirring once, 45 to 55 minutes or until vegetables are tender and deep golden at the edges.

4. Sprinkle with feta and basil (if using) and serve.

Make ahead Roast the vegetables but don't add the cheese and basil. Keep at room temperature for up to 4 hours. Reheat at 425°F for 5 to 10 minutes, then finish with the cheese and basil.

Prep Time 15 minutes
Ready In a little over 1 hour

1 small red onion, sliced into ¼-inch rings

2 Japanese eggplants, cut into large cubes

2 sweet red peppers, cut into wedges

2 zucchini, cut into ½-inch rounds

¼ cup extra-virgin olive oil

2 tablespoons balsamic vinegar

½ teaspoon salt

½ cup crumbled feta cheese (optional)

Fresh basil leaves (optional)

French Potato Salad

Serves 6 to 8 • Make ahead

Prep Time 15 minutes or less
Ready In about 45 minutes

3 pounds (1.35 kg) red-skinned potatoes (6 to 8 medium potatoes)

3 tablespoons grainy Dijon mustard

2 teaspoons regular Dijon mustard

⅓ cup red wine vinegar

1 shallot, finely chopped

2 teaspoons granulated sugar

½ teaspoon salt

½ cup canola oil

2 tablespoons chopped fresh parsley

Fresh black pepper

This is the best potato salad. It ticks all the boxes for potato salad—easy, tangy, delicious—without being creamy or heavy in any way. It even seems to improve after a day in the fridge. It's simple but sophisticated and everyone just loves it. The shallot is important: I have tried this with regular onions and green onions, and it's not as good. Serve with Soy and Garlic Grilled Flank Steak (page 95), Maple-Garlic Cedar Salmon (page 232) or Slow-Cooker Sweet and Spicy Ribs (page 106).

1. Scrub the potatoes, then cut them in halves (or quarters if large). Place them in a large pot and cover with cold water. Season the water generously with salt, then bring to a boil. Reduce heat and boil gently 15 to 20 minutes or until the potatoes are completely tender. Drain.

2. Meanwhile, whisk the grainy and regular mustards with red wine vinegar in a large bowl. Whisk in the shallot, sugar and salt. Gradually add the canola oil, whisking constantly until emulsified.

3. Add the warm potatoes and the parsley to the dressing and stir gently to combine. Season with pepper. Let stand until room temperature, or chill before serving.

Make ahead Make the potato salad, without the parsley, up to 1 day in advance. Stir in the parsley just before serving.

Greek Orzo Salad with Basil

Serves 10 • Make ahead

One of my recipe testers said of this salad, "I can never make this again—I ate the entire batch myself. Seriously." I know the feeling! And every time I serve this salad, someone asks me for the recipe. It's funny how the simplest dishes sometimes have the most impact, but somehow the whole of this salad is greater than the sum of its parts. This is really just a good pasta salad, but orzo takes it up a level, and the olives, tomatoes and goat cheese make it something quite special. It lasts very well in the fridge, too. I serve this with anything from Lemony Lamb Chops (page 109) to Maple-Garlic Cedar Salmon (page 232) to Naked Burgers (page 100).

Prep Time 20 minutes or less
Ready In about 25 minutes

1 pound (450 g) orzo pasta (about 2 cups)

2 tablespoons white wine vinegar

1 teaspoon Dijon mustard

½ teaspoon salt

⅓ cup extra-virgin olive oil

1 cup Kalamata olives, pitted and coarsely chopped

8 oil-packed sun-dried tomatoes, drained and thinly sliced

Fresh black pepper

4 ounces (115 g) plain soft goat cheese (about ⅓ cup), crumbled

12 fresh basil leaves, thinly sliced

1. Boil orzo in a pot of salted water until just barely tender, 6 to 8 minutes or according to package directions. Drain, then rinse with running water until cold.

2. Whisk white wine vinegar with mustard and salt in a large bowl. Whisk in the olive oil until combined. Whisk in the olives and tomatoes. Stir in the orzo. Season with pepper. Stir in the goat cheese and basil.

Make ahead Make the salad but don't add the goat cheese or basil. Keep in the fridge for up to 1 day. Stir in the cheese and basil just before serving.

Switch it up Add 1 pint of cherry tomatoes, halved, or 4 cups of baby arugula (or both) just before serving.

Easy Maple-Mustard Ham
Serves 6 to 10

Prep Time 5 minutes or less
Ready In about 75 minutes

1 fully cooked bone-in smoked ham (5½ pounds/ 2.5 kg) (see Tip), usually called a quarter ham

2 tablespoons Dijon mustard

2 teaspoons pure maple syrup

Tip 1. A bone-in ham is the kind of thing that you should pre-order from a good local butcher. Call a week in advance to make sure you get one. **2.** To serve 16 to 25, buy a half ham (about 11 pounds/5 kg). To serve 40 to 50 people, buy a whole ham (about 18 to 22 pounds/8 to 10 kg). Bake about 10 minutes per pound. **3.** Slice only as much as you are serving at one time (big pieces have a longer shelf life). Cool completely in the fridge. Large chunks can be wrapped well in plastic wrap, then popped into a large resealable plastic bag and frozen for up to 2 months. Use up refrigerated smaller pieces within 5 days.

When our son, Thomas, turned one, we felt compelled to really celebrate. Getting through the first twelve months without anyone being accidentally abandoned somewhere was cause for a party. We recklessly invited fifty people. I fretted about fitting so many guests into our minuscule house, about the cake, about the trap door in our kitchen floor leading to the basement (we called it the death-trap door, although it ultimately took no victims). But I never worried about the food: I served a ham.

Ham is the easiest roast for any kind of party, from a formal Easter dinner with in-laws to a casual neighbourhood open house for forty or more. The genius thing about a good ham is that it's already fully cooked, relieving you from the stress of cooking it "just right." All you're doing is heating it up. Children love ham—that in itself is reason to put it on the menu—and adults do too. It's an old-fashioned taste that somehow takes guests by surprise and delights them. Plus, there are plenty of divine leftovers for sandwiches and omelettes, on top of pancakes or waffles, simmered in pea soups or just tucked into the freezer for a last-minute meal.

For a casual party, serve the ham with soft white buns, dishes of butter, sweet and hot mustards, Cucumber Fridge Pickles (page 204) and sliced cucumber so guests can make sandwiches at their leisure. For a sit-down dinner, serve with Make-Ahead Scalloped Potatoes (page 227) and Curried Cauliflower and Cheddar Gratin (page 231).

....

1. Preheat the oven to 300°F. Line a medium roasting pan with foil.

2. Dry the ham with paper towels and place it cut side down in the prepared pan (no rack required). Cover loosely with foil. Bake 55 to 60 minutes, or until a thermometer inserted as far into the ham as possible reads at least 140°F.

3. Take off the foil, stir the mustard and maple syrup together, then smear the mixture all over the ham. Bake 15 to 20 more minutes, uncovered, until glaze firms up a bit.

4. Serve warm or at room temperature, thinly sliced.

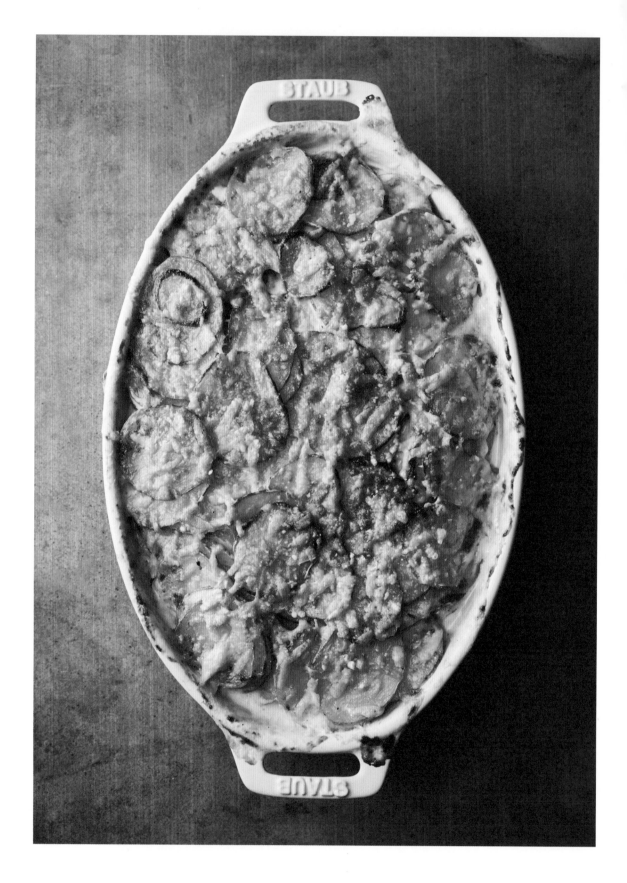

Make-Ahead Scalloped Potatoes

Serves 8 to 10 • Make ahead

The trouble with traditional scalloped potatoes—as I used to see it—is that they go into the oven raw, and then take an age to cook. In the old days I would poke them again and again, hoping they'd be tender before the pan got dry. So frustrating. But the solution is to par-cook the potatoes (and as a bonus, cook them in cream!) or even pre-cook the whole dish.

Yukon Golds are my go-to all-purpose potato, but you can use any yellow-fleshed variety here. I don't peel my potatoes, but if you'd prefer a perfectly smooth dish, then go right ahead. It won't change the cooking time. These are terrific with Dry-Brined Turkey (page 213), Easy Maple-Mustard Ham (page 224), Soy and Garlic Grilled Flank Steak (page 95) or Herb and Garlic Meatloaf (page 91).

1. Preheat the oven to 400°F. Grease a 9- x 13-inch baking dish (or other 12- to 14-cup baking dish) with butter.

2. Scrub the potatoes, then slice them very thinly—about ⅛ inch—or run them through a mandoline (see Tip). The important thing here is to make the slices the same thickness. Place the slices in a large pot. Sprinkle in the salt and garlic, then pour in the cream and milk. Season with pepper. Bring to a gentle boil over medium heat, stirring gently. Boil gently for 2 minutes.

3. Transfer the mixture to the prepared baking dish, arranging the potatoes in an even layer. The cream mixture should be just below the level of the potatoes. Place the dish on a rimmed baking sheet to catch any spill-over. Sprinkle with the Parmesan.

4. Bake 35 to 40 minutes or until bubbly and browned. Check after about 25 minutes, and if the top is getting quite brown, tent the dish with foil for the remaining cooking time.

Tip A mandoline is a slicing gadget. You can find inexpensive plastic ones in kitchenware shops. Make sure to use the finger guard every time! If your food processor has a slicing blade, that's fine here as well, but if it has variable thickness do not use the thinnest setting. Slices shouldn't be thinner than ⅛ inch.

Prep Time 20 minutes
Ready In a little over 1 hour

1 tablespoon butter

3 pounds (1.35 kg) Yukon Gold potatoes (about 7 medium potatoes)

¾ teaspoon salt

1 large clove garlic, chopped

1 cup whipping (35%) cream or table (18%) cream

1 cup 2% milk

Fresh black pepper

1 cup freshly grated Parmesan cheese

Make ahead Fully bake the dish, then cool to room temperature. Cover and keep in the fridge for up to 1 day. Cover with foil and reheat at 400°F for about 20 minutes, then take off the foil and bake another 5 to 10 minutes until hot.

Chicken with Garlic and Prunes

Serves 4

Prep Time 15 minutes or less
Ready In about 1 hour

1 whole chicken (about
3 pounds/1.35 kg),
spatchcocked (see Tip)

½ teaspoon salt, divided

1 tablespoon canola oil

¾ cup pitted prunes

10 small cloves garlic, not
peeled

10 sprigs fresh thyme

1 cup dry white wine

Tip To flatten, or
spatchcock, the chicken
yourself, use strong kitchen
scissors to cut along each
side of the backbone to
remove it (freeze it for Slow-
Cooker Chicken Stock,
page 67). Flip the chicken
over and press down firmly
on the breastbone so the
chicken lies flat (think of it
like giving the bird CPR).
Most butchers sell chickens
pre-flattened, or will do it
for you if you ask.

This is a mash-up of my two favourite chicken recipes for entertaining. The first, chicken with 40 cloves of garlic, is one of the first recipes I ever truly mastered, and the one that showed me just how magical garlic can really be when it's slowly cooked whole. The second, chicken Marbella, is one of the world's most famous dishes. Marbella is a genius make-ahead party dish combining prunes, olives, brown sugar and white wine, and it's delicious hot or cold.

Both recipes originally call for a whole chicken broken down into eight pieces. Simply spatchcocking the bird—or buying it pre-flattened—is faster and makes for easier browning and a pretty presentation. I love this dish for a small dinner party, served with lots of good bread (the juices are incredible), Roasted Broccoli with Lemon and Parmesan (page 188) or Celery and Fennel Salad (page 178) or just a big green salad. Add an uncomplicated dessert or a little box of chocolates and you've got a fantastic, easy dinner party.

••

1. Dry the chicken well with paper towels, then sprinkle the skin side with ¼ teaspoon of the salt.

2. Heat a large frying pan (one with a lid) over medium-high heat. Add the canola oil. When it's hot, add the chicken, skin side down, and sprinkle with the remaining ¼ teaspoon salt. Cook 5 minutes.

3. Carefully turn the chicken over (I use a spatula and a pair of tongs), and then scatter the prunes, garlic and thyme sprigs around it. Pour in the white wine. Reduce the heat to medium-low, cover and cook 35 to 40 minutes or until the chicken is cooked through (a thermometer inserted into the thickest part of the thigh should read 175°F). Carefully transfer the chicken to a cutting board to rest.

4. Bring the pan sauce to a boil. Boil 5 minutes or until reduced and slightly thickened. Remove and discard the thyme sprigs. Cut chicken into pieces and serve with sauce, garlic and prunes.

Curried Cauliflower and Cheddar Gratin

Serves 10 • Make ahead

I'm always trying to come up with vegetable side dishes for entertaining that can be made in advance. When I'm hosting a dinner party, I try to have everything but one dish finished ahead of time so I can enjoy the party instead of scrambling around in the kitchen trying to get everything done at once. You can do all the work for this recipe early in the day, then just pop the pan in the oven shortly before you serve dinner. The combination of curry, cauliflower and Cheddar is a knockout! Serve this with Easy Maple-Mustard Ham (page 224), Weekday Roast Chicken (page 65) or Rosemary-Roasted Pork Tenderloin (page 103).

Prep Time 20 minutes
Ready In about 45 minutes

2 small heads cauliflower

2 cups panko crumbs

½ cup butter, melted

1 tablespoon mild curry powder

1 cup grated old Cheddar cheese

¼ teaspoon salt

1. Bring a large pot of well-salted water to a boil. Meanwhile, cut the cauliflower into medium-sized florets. Drop into the boiling water. Once the water returns to a rolling boil, cook 2 to 3 minutes or until the cauliflower is just fork-tender (it will soften just a bit more in the oven). Drain and let cool to room temperature.

2. Preheat the oven to 400°F. Grease a 9- x 13-inch baking dish with a little butter or non-stick cooking spray (see page 4).

3. Combine the panko with melted butter and curry powder in a medium bowl. Stir well, then stir in the cheese until well mixed. Place the cauliflower in the prepared baking dish. It should fit snugly in a single layer; if not, just nestle all the florets close to each other in the centre of the baking dish. Sprinkle evenly with salt, then with the panko mixture.

4. Bake 16 to 20 minutes or until golden and crunchy. Let stand 5 minutes before serving.

Make ahead Assemble the dish but do not bake. Keep at room temperature for up to 4 hours or in the fridge for up to 8 hours. Bake as per the recipe, increasing the bake time by 5 to 10 minutes if you've kept the dish in the fridge.

Maple-Garlic Cedar Salmon
Serves 6 • Make ahead

Prep Time 10 minutes or less
Ready In a little over 1 hour

1 untreated cedar plank
(about 12 inches long)

1 skin-on centre-cut salmon
fillet (2¼ pounds/1 kg)

2 tablespoons pure maple
syrup

1 tablespoon canola oil

½ teaspoon garlic powder

1 red onion, thinly sliced

½ teaspoon salt

Salmon is a wonderful, versatile fish as is, but this recipe might be its finest hour. The grilled cedar lightly smokes the fish from below while the maple, garlic and onion flavour it from the top. The fish stays juicy and moist. Heaven! This is my go-to dish for elegant summer entertaining, and I usually grill it an hour or so before the party starts and serve it at room temperature. This salmon with French Potato Salad (page 220), Grilled Corn (page 185) and Celery and Fennel Salad (page 178) is one of my favourite summer menus.

1. Soak the cedar plank in cold water for at least 30 minutes but up to 8 hours. (I put mine in a big roasting pan full of water and weigh it down with two cans from the pantry.)

2. Preheat the grill to medium-high heat. Take the plank out of the water and place the salmon on it, skin side down. Cut the salmon into 6 portions, slicing all the way through the flesh but not through the skin.

3. Stir the maple syrup with canola oil and garlic powder. Smear this mixture all over the salmon, including into the cuts. Sprinkle the onion evenly over the top, then sprinkle everything with the salt.

4. Place the salmon and plank on the grill. Close the lid and cook for 20 to 25 minutes or until the salmon is firm but springy to the touch. There will be tiny ridges of white protein along the edges of the fish, a sign that the fish is cooked.

5. Take the plank off the grill. Slide a thin spatula between the skin and the salmon to release and serve each fillet.

Tip You can also use 6 evenly sized skin-on salmon fillets instead of a whole side.

Make ahead Grill the salmon and chill, covered loosely with plastic wrap, for up to 24 hours. Serve chilled.

Baking

Chocolate Fudge Layer Cake

Makes one 9-inch round two-layer cake • Serves 8 to 10 • Make ahead

A few years ago, my birthday came along during a really busy time for our family. I can't remember the details, but suffice to say it was the morning of my birthday and I wasn't sure Michael would be baking a cake that day. I was up early, I love to bake, so I decided to make my own. Not wanting to turn on the mixer and wake the household, I came up with a chocolate cake that you can mix with just a bowl and spoon. The cocoa powder makes this very fudgy, while the canola oil (used instead of butter) makes the cake both fluffy and moist.

This is not an overly sweet cake. Once it's frosted, I find the flavour balance to be just right, but if you prefer your cake a little sweeter, increase the sugar by ½ cup.

1. Preheat the oven to 350°F. Grease two 9-inch round cake pans with non-stick baking spray (see page 4).

2. To make the Chocolate Fudge Cake, whisk the flour with the sugar, cocoa powder, baking soda, baking powder and salt in a large bowl. In a small bowl, whisk the egg, then whisk in milk, canola oil and vanilla. Pour the egg mixture into the flour mixture and stir to combine. Add the water and stir until well combined.

3. Scrape the batter into the prepared pans. Firmly tap each pan on the counter once to release any large air bubbles. Bake 35 to 45 minutes or until a cake tester inserted into the centre comes out clean. Let cool 5 minutes, then flip out onto racks to cool completely before frosting.

4. To make the Vanilla Frosting, beat the butter with icing sugar using an electric mixer on medium speed. Beat in the milk and vanilla, then increase speed to high and beat until very smooth and fluffy.

5. Stack cake layers on top of each other, using about one-quarter of the frosting in between the layers. Use the remaining frosting to cover the top and sides.

Tip An offset spatula is an inexpensive piece of equipment that makes frosting cakes much easier. Spoon the frosting onto the cake, then use the offset spatula to swoosh it around decoratively.

Prep Time 25 minutes
Ready In about 2 hours

Chocolate Fudge Cake

2½ cups (370 g) all-purpose flour

2 cups (410 g) granulated sugar

1⅓ cups (130 g) unsweetened cocoa powder

2½ teaspoons baking soda

1 teaspoon baking powder

1 teaspoon salt

1 egg

1⅓ cups milk

⅔ cup canola oil

1 teaspoon pure vanilla extract

1 cup warm water

Vanilla Frosting

1 cup (225 g) butter, at room temperature

6 cups (660 g) icing sugar

¼ cup 2% milk or whipping (35%) cream

2 teaspoons pure vanilla extract

Make ahead Make and frost the cake up to 1 day in advance. Or bake the cakes and let them cool completely. Wrap with two layers of plastic wrap and freeze for up to 2 weeks. Assemble and frost the frozen cake layers and let the cake thaw fully at room temperature.

Gingerbread Bundt Cake with Lemon Glaze

Makes one 10-inch bundt • Serves 12 • Make ahead

Prep Time 15 minutes or less
Ready In about 1½ hours

Gingerbread Bundt

3⅓ cups (500 g) all-purpose flour

1 tablespoon ground ginger

2 teaspoons cinnamon

2 teaspoons baking soda

1½ teaspoons salt

2 eggs

1 cup canola oil

¾ cup (155 g) granulated sugar

1 cup (330 g) molasses

1 cup hot water

Lemon Glaze

1½ cups (170 g) icing sugar

¼ cup fresh lemon juice

Although we tend to associate gingerbread with Christmas, this cake is welcome year-round, and particularly on lazy weekends when everyone stays in their pyjamas until noon. This cake looks and tastes spectacular, so it's good enough for company, or even a birthday party.

Bundt cakes are especially simple since they don't need to be frosted to look gorgeous; in fact, frosting them would be a nightmare! This glazed beauty was inspired by a gorgeous bundt pan I was given several years ago; any cake baked in it gets rave reviews.

....

1. Preheat the oven to 325°F. Spray a 10 cup Bundt pan generously with non-stick baking spray (see page 4).

2. To make the Gingerbread Bundt, whisk the flour with ginger, cinnamon, baking soda and salt in a large bowl. In a separate bowl, whisk the eggs well. Whisk in canola oil, then sugar and molasses. Pour the egg mixture into the flour mixture and stir well. Add hot water and stir well.

3. Scrape the batter into the prepared pan. Bake 55 minutes or until a cake tester inserted into the centre comes out clean. Let cool in the pan on a rack 10 minutes.

4. To make the Lemon Glaze, whisk the icing sugar with the lemon juice until smooth.

5. Flip the cake out onto a rack set over a baking sheet. Let cake cool for another 5 minutes, then poke deep holes all over the cake using a long skewer. Drizzle glaze all over cake, trying to get some into each hole, and brushing the glaze so it covers the entire surface of the cake. Serve warm or let cool completely.

Tip Always buy fancy molasses for baking. Cooking molasses is too bitter for cakes.

Make ahead Make and glaze the cake up to 1 day in advance of serving. Store at room temperature.

Buttery Vanilla Cake with Chocolate Cream Cheese Frosting

Makes one 8-inch square cake • Serves 9 • Make ahead

If I have a signature dessert, this is it. Every time I serve it, someone asks for the recipe. Part of the cake's appeal is its simplicity. The recipe calls for just ⅓ cup of butter and one egg, plus a few other pantry staples, and it doesn't need to be made in a mixer. But it's also a knockout in terms of flavour, and the edges get deeply caramelized and almost crunchy. It's so versatile, too. Here it's a humble single-layer square cake, but you can also bake this batter into a dozen cupcakes, or in a 9-inch round pan, or double the recipe, bake it in two pans and make it into a celebratory layer cake. It also keeps remarkably well just on the counter. But be warned: you might find yourself slicing off a thin piece every time you walk by the pan (okay, maybe that's just me).

1. Preheat the oven to 350°F. Grease an 8-inch square baking dish well with non-stick baking spray (see page 4).

2. To make the Buttery Vanilla Cake, beat the butter and sugar together, by hand or using an electric mixer on medium speed, until well combined. Beat in the egg and vanilla until well combined. Add the flour, baking powder and salt, and stir gently until just combined. Add the milk and stir well.

3. Scrape the batter into the prepared pan. Bake 25 to 30 minutes or until golden and a cake tester inserted into the centre comes out clean. Let cool in the pan on a rack 10 minutes, then flip out onto a rack to cool completely before frosting.

4. To make Chocolate Cream Cheese Frosting, beat the cream cheese and butter together until smooth and fluffy (by hand or in a mixer). Add the icing sugar all at once and stir until combined. Stir in vanilla. Scrape in all the chocolate and beat until fluffy, scraping the sides of the bowl as needed. Spread over the cooled cake.

Make ahead Bake and cool the cake completely. Wrap very well with at least two layers of plastic wrap then freeze for up to 1 week. Make frosting and keep refrigerated for up to 2 days. Let the frosting come to room temperature before applying to the cake. The cake can be frosted while frozen and left at room temperature to thaw, about 2 hours.

Prep Time 15 minutes
Ready In about 2 hours

Buttery Vanilla Cake

⅓ cup (85 g) butter, at room temperature

1 cup (205 g) granulated sugar

1 egg

1 teaspoon pure vanilla extract

1⅓ cups (195 g) all-purpose flour

2 teaspoons baking powder

½ teaspoon salt

⅔ cup milk

Chocolate Cream Cheese Frosting

125 g (half an 8-ounce/250 g package) cream cheese, at room temperature

¼ cup (60 g) butter, at room temperature

2 cups (220 g) icing sugar

½ teaspoon pure vanilla extract

2 squares (2 ounces/60 g) semi-sweet chocolate, melted and cooled

One-Bowl Carrot Cake

Makes one 9-inch round two-layer cake • Serves 8 to 10 • Make ahead

Prep Time 20 minutes
Ready In about 2 hours

Carrot Cake

1½ cups (325 g) granulated sugar

¾ cup (180 g) butter, melted

2 teaspoons cinnamon

1 teaspoon freshly grated nutmeg

1 teaspoon salt

1 teaspoon pure vanilla extract

Zest of 1 orange

4 eggs

2 cups (300 g) all-purpose flour

2 teaspoons baking powder

1 teaspoon baking soda

2½ cups (240 g) grated carrots (about 3 large carrots)

1 cup (140 g) dried cranberries

1 cup (110 g) chopped toasted walnuts

Cream Cheese Frosting

1 package (8 ounces/250 g) cream cheese, at room temperature

½ cup (115 g) butter, at room temperature

4 cups (440 g) icing sugar

1 tablespoon fresh lemon or orange juice

1 teaspoon pure vanilla extract

This is the cake I made for my sister's wedding. (Offering to make a three-tiered cake for a wedding taking place in the woods when I was also the maid of honour remains one of my most foolish life decisions.) The wedding day was sweltering hot and humid. When I started to frost the layers at the venue, the buttercream began melting right off the cake. Then, when I added the supporting dowels and placed the second tier on top of the first, the entire thing slid sideways. Cue panic! I was glad the lights were dimmed when my sister and her husband cut into it. And there wasn't a crumb left at the end of the night.

It was a complicated moment for me, but this cake is the best kind of uncomplicated. It comes together quickly and in just one bowl, but it's packed with flavour, and the orange zest and cranberries take it over the top.

....

1. Preheat the oven to 350°F. Spray two 9-inch round cake pans with non-stick baking spray (see page 4).

2. To make the Carrot Cake, stir the sugar and butter together in a large bowl. Stir in the cinnamon, nutmeg, salt, vanilla and orange zest. Stir in the eggs until well combined. Add the flour, baking powder and baking soda and stir well to combine. Stir in the carrots, cranberries and walnuts.

3. Divide the batter evenly between the prepared pans and smooth the tops. Bake 30 to 35 minutes or until a cake tester inserted into the centre comes out mostly clean with a few crumbs still sticking to it. Let cool in the pans on racks 10 minutes, then flip out onto racks to cool completely.

4. To make the Cream Cheese Frosting, beat the cream cheese and butter together until smooth and fluffy (by hand or in a mixer). Add the icing sugar all at once and stir until combined. Stir in the lemon juice and vanilla and beat until fluffy.

5. Place one cake layer on a cake plate and top with about half of the frosting. Spread it right to the edge, then place the second layer on top. Frost the top, leaving the sides bare.

Make ahead Make and frost the cake up to 1 day in advance. Or bake the cakes and let them cool completely. Wrap with two layers of plastic wrap and freeze for up to 2 weeks. Assemble and frost the frozen cake layers and let the cake thaw fully at room temperature.

Raspberry Shortcakes

Makes 4 individual shortcakes • Make ahead

Shortcakes are a great way to show off whatever fruit is in season. Raspberries are my favourite berry, but these are equally pretty and delicious stuffed with blueberries, sliced strawberries or peaches.

These little cakes are a lot like scones, but lighter and easier to make since they call for cream and no butter. I often use half whole wheat flour and add a handful of raisins to the dough and serve them for brunch.

....

1. Preheat the oven to 425°F. Line a rimmed baking sheet with parchment paper.

2. To make the Shortcakes, stir the flour, sugar, baking powder and salt together in a large bowl. Add the cream and stir until combined. If the dough is still very dry, add 1 to 2 tablespoons more cream.

3. Transfer to a lightly floured counter and shape into a circle. It's okay to knead it a bit to make the shape even. Cut into 4 wedges and transfer them to the prepared baking sheet, leaving lots of space in between the wedges.

4. If you like, brush tops with a little water, then sprinkle with coarse sugar. Bake 12 to 15 minutes or until golden. Transfer to a rack to cool completely.

5. To make the Raspberry Topping, stir raspberries with 1 tablespoon of the sugar and let stand 10 minutes. Whip the cream with the remaining 2 tablespoons sugar until it holds soft peaks.

6. Slice each shortcake in half and place them on 4 plates. Fill each one with whipped cream and raspberries. Drizzle cream with any juices from the raspberry bowl.

Make ahead Baked shortcakes keep well, wrapped at room temperature, for up to 1 day.

Switch it up 1. In place of fresh, use 2 cups frozen raspberries stirred with 1 to 2 tablespoons sugar and left to thaw for 2 hours on the counter. **2.** Add the zest of 1 lemon or orange to the shortcake batter, along with the cream.

Prep Time 15 minutes
Ready In about 1 hour

Shortcakes

1 cup (150 g) all-purpose flour

2 tablespoons granulated sugar

2 teaspoons baking powder

¼ teaspoon salt

⅔ cup whipping (35%) cream

1 tablespoon coarse sugar (optional)

Raspberry Topping

2 cups (250 g) raspberries

3 tablespoons granulated sugar, divided

⅔ cup whipping (35%) cream

No-Bake Coconut Cream Cake

Makes one 8-inch loaf • Serves 4 to 6 • Make ahead

Prep Time 15 minutes
Ready In a little over 6 hours

1½ cups whipping (35%) cream

¼ cup (50 g) granulated sugar

2 teaspoons coconut extract

½ cup light rum

40 plain vanilla wafer cookies (such as Nilla)

½ cup (50 g) sweetened flaked coconut, toasted

Refrigerator cakes (also known as ice-box cakes) are wonderful, easy creations perfect for when you don't have the will or energy to bake, whether that's a busy weeknight or a blisteringly hot summer day. Vanilla, cream, rum and coconut are a match made in cocktail heaven, and the combination transfers deliciously to dessert.

....

1. Line an 8- x 4-inch loaf pan with 2 sheets of plastic wrap, leaving some wrap over-hanging the long sides.

2. Whip the cream with the sugar and coconut extract using an electric mixer on high speed until it holds soft peaks. Spread about ¾ cup of the whipped cream evenly over the bottom of the prepared pan.

3. Place the rum in a small dish. Quickly dip 8 cookies into the rum, then place them in 2 rows on top of the cream in the pan. Top with about ½ cup of the whipped cream and spread evenly to the edges of the pan.

4. Repeat the layers, ending with a layer of cookies and drizzling with any remaining rum. Fold the overhanging plastic wrap over the top and refrigerate at least 6 hours or up to 24 hours.

5. To serve, unfold the plastic wrap, then place a serving platter over the pan. Flip the pan and platter upside down, remove the pan and gently lift off the plastic wrap. Sprinkle with toasted coconut. Slice thickly to serve.

Tip To toast coconut, spread it in a medium non-stick frying pan over medium heat. Cook, stirring frequently, until golden. Take it out of the pan (or it will keep cooking).

Make ahead Assemble the cake and keep it in the fridge for up to 1 day before serving.

Switch it up If you are serving children, replace the rum with an equal amount of coconut water or unsweetened apple juice.

Black Forest Brownie Cookies

Makes 24 cookies • Make ahead

I call these my "secret-weapon cookies." When I was first working as a freelance writer, I would include a little packet of these with story pitches to editors. I figured they showed off my real live cooking skills and made my story pitch stand out from competitors. Also, fudgy cookies stuffed with boozy cherries make everyone happy. I don't think they got me too many writing gigs, but at least I perfected the recipe.

I love using cocoa powder in baked goods. It adds so much richness without the fuss of chopping and melting chocolate.

···

1. Position racks in the upper and lower thirds of the oven. Preheat the oven to 350°F. Line 2 baking sheets with parchment paper.

2. Combine the cherries and brandy in a small bowl and microwave for 30 seconds. If you're using hot water, just combine the two ingredients and let stand.

3. Whisk the flour with the cocoa, baking soda and salt in a medium bowl. In a separate large bowl, beat the butter with the brown sugar until light and fluffy. Add the egg and vanilla and beat until well combined. Add the flour mixture and stir until combined. Stir in chocolate chips and the cherries, plus any unabsorbed liquid.

4. Scoop dough into balls (rolled with about 2 level tablespoons each) and place about 2 inches apart on the prepared baking sheets. Bake, switching sheets on racks halfway, 9 to 12 minutes or until tops are just firm. Transfer to a rack to cool completely.

Make ahead Scoop the raw cookie dough into balls, then freeze in a single layer on a baking sheet. Once completely frozen, transfer the balls to a resealable plastic bag and keep frozen for up to 1 month. Thaw at room temperature before baking.

Prep Time 20 minutes
Ready In a little over ½ hour
(if you like warm cookies)

¾ cup (100 g) dried sweet cherries

2 tablespoons brandy or hot water

1 cup (150 g) all-purpose flour

½ cup (45 g) unsweetened cocoa powder

½ teaspoon baking soda

¼ teaspoon salt

½ cup (115 g) butter, at room temperature

¾ cup (165 g) packed brown sugar

1 egg

1 teaspoon pure vanilla extract

¾ cup (130 g) semi-sweet or dark chocolate chips

Chocolate Chip Cookies

Makes 24 cookies • Make ahead • Batch cooking

Prep Time 20 minutes
Ready In a little over ½ hour
(for warm cookies)

1½ cups (225 g) all-purpose flour

½ teaspoon baking soda

¼ teaspoon salt

½ cup (115 g) butter, at room temperature

¾ cup (165 g) packed brown sugar

1 egg

2 teaspoons pure vanilla extract

1½ cups (260 g) semi-sweet or dark chocolate chips

Years ago I worked as a chef in the test kitchen of a major grocery brand. It was a fascinating, fun job, and developing recipes for packaging was what I loved most. One day I was asked to develop a foolproof recipe to showcase a new kind of chocolate chip, and I had less than two square inches on the package for the ingredients and full recipe in both English and French. So I took my favourite recipe and started testing, omitting ingredients and streamlining the method. Finally, I had a six-ingredient cookie recipe with a two-sentence method. I'm exhausted just thinking about it! In the years since, I've kept tinkering with it, reducing the sugar and adding vanilla. The recipe has grown a bit, but it's the ideal cookie: just the right balance between crisp and chewy. These cookies are shown on page 248.

1. Position racks in the upper and lower thirds of the oven. Preheat the oven to 350°F. Line 2 baking sheets with parchment paper.

2. Whisk the flour with baking soda and salt in a medium bowl. In a separate large bowl, use a wooden spoon or an electric mixer to mix the butter with the brown sugar until light and fluffy. Mix in the egg and vanilla until well combined. Add the flour mixture and stir until combined. Stir in the chocolate chips.

3. Scoop dough into balls (rolled with about 2 level tablespoons each) and place about 2 inches apart on the prepared baking sheets. Bake, switching sheets on racks halfway, 9 to 12 minutes or until just done, golden at the edges but not all the way across the top. Transfer to a rack to cool completely.

Tip Make these even more special by using chopped best-quality chocolate in place of the chocolate chips. This way each cookie is crammed with a mix of big hunks and little shards of melty chocolate. I use Lindt 70% bars, which are thin and easy to chop.

Make ahead Scoop the raw cookie dough into balls, then freeze in a single layer on a baking sheet. Once completely frozen, transfer the balls to a resealable plastic bag and keep frozen for up to 1 month. Thaw at room temperature before baking.

Batch cooking This recipe doubles well. Freeze the dough in balls (see Make ahead), then bake as many or as few at a time as you like.

Forgiving Food Processor Pastry

Makes enough pastry for one 9-inch single-crust pie • Make ahead • Batch cooking

Pastry sounds daunting. Many cooks who easily conquer complicated cakes, squares and cookies still balk at pastry. That's how I felt until my twenties, when I discovered it can be made without heartache or too much time. I was working at a busy gourmet shop that sold pie by the slice. We made lots and lots of cream cheese pastry, which rolls out beautifully and lasts well after it's cooked. There's no water, vinegar or egg, and the cream cheese gives the pastry structure and flexibility. This pastry is wonderfully forgiving, and can be over-worked without getting tough (as butter or lard pastry can). Use it for any sweet or savoury recipes. Try a Plum-Almond Galette (page 255), Rhubarb and Apple Pie (page 256) or Chocolate Silk Pie (page 252).

....

1. Combine flour and salt in the food processor. Pulse to combine.

2. Add cream cheese and butter, and pulse for 30 seconds to 1 minute or until the dough comes together in a loose ball.

3. Shape the dough into a flat disc about 1 inch thick. Wrap in plastic wrap and chill at least 30 minutes before using.

4. To use the pastry, leave it at room temperature until it's pliable enough to roll. Depending on the weather this can take 30 minutes (summer) or 3 hours (winter). If frozen, thaw it in the fridge first, then leave on the counter until pliable.

Make ahead Pastry can be made and frozen, wrapped in a resealable plastic bag, for up to 2 months.

Batch cooking Most food processors can easily handle a double batch. Divide the pastry in half and wrap each disc individually.

Prep Time 10 minutes
Ready In about 40 minutes

1½ cups (225 g) all-purpose flour

⅛ teaspoon salt

½ cup (115 g) cream cheese, cold and cubed

½ cup (115 g) butter, cold and cubed

Chocolate Silk Pie

Makes one 9-inch pie • Serves 8

Prep Time 25 minutes or less
Ready In about 90 minutes if
pastry is made

1 batch Forgiving Food
Processor Pastry (page 251)

1 box (113 g) instant
chocolate pudding mix

2 cups 2% milk

1 cup whipping (35%) cream

2 tablespoons granulated
sugar

Tip To make fancy
chocolate curls, microwave
a bar of good-quality dark
chocolate for 10 to 20
seconds. Working over the
pie, run a vegetable peeler
along the edge to create
chocolate curls, letting the
curls fall randomly.

This is one of my favourite desserts from my childhood. My mom made pie almost every Sunday, but this was a cheat in her eyes—a pie not good enough for company because it uses packaged pudding. We didn't care, because it meant more for us!

What I thought was a Tansey family invention is actually a real dessert called chocolate silk pie. Its combination of crisp pastry with cool chocolate filling and oodles of sweet whipped cream is delightful. The "real" version would use homemade pudding, but Mom's version is so good I just don't see the point. The pastry, however, has to be from scratch, and the whipped cream too—otherwise it's too sweet and the pie becomes unbalanced. Unlike Mom, I've served this to guests countless times, and they always declare it to be the best pie they've ever eaten. I know the pastry part sounds complicated, but it only takes 5 minutes.

....

1. Preheat the oven to 425°F.

2. Roll out the pastry on a lightly floured counter, using a lightly floured rolling pin, until it's roughly a 13-inch circle. Loosen the pastry from the counter by gently sliding a thin metal spatula underneath it, then transfer to a 9-inch pie plate. Gently press the pastry into the pie plate. Trim off the excess pastry, leaving about ½ inch overhang, then fold the edges towards the centre and crimp by gently pressing between your thumb and index finger. Prick the bottom of the pastry all over with a fork. Tear off a large square of parchment paper and press it into the pie shell. Fill it with dried beans or pie weights.

3. Bake the bean-filled pie shell for 15 minutes or until the crimped edge is just barely golden. Take the whole pie out of the oven and lift out the parchment with the beans. Put the shell back into the oven and bake another 5 to 7 minutes or until it's golden all across the bottom. Let cool to room temperature.

4. Mix up the pudding with the milk according to package directions and immediately pour it into the cooled shell. Pop it all into the fridge to chill, about 30 minutes.

5. Shortly before serving, whip the cream with the sugar until it holds soft peaks (1 minute in a stand mixer, 2 minutes with an electric hand mixer). Dollop the whipped cream over the chilled pie and serve immediately.

Plum-Almond Galette

Makes one 10-inch galette • Serves 8 • Make ahead

Galette is pie at its most simple. The free-form shape means it's easy to make, but still so pretty once baked. This is my favourite way to use late-summer stone fruit like peaches, nectarines and plums, because their colour and shape make for a stunning and equally delicious galette. I've kept the sugar quite low for the filling—it's best to taste the plums first and add another ¼ cup or so of sugar if they aren't quite as sweet.

....

1. Preheat the oven to 425°F. Line a large rimmed baking sheet with parchment paper.

2. Roll out the pastry on a lightly floured counter, using a lightly floured rolling pin, into a 14-inch circle. Loosen the pastry from the counter by gently sliding a thin metal spatula underneath it, then transfer to the prepared baking sheet.

3. Pit the plums and slice each one into 6 to 8 wedges. You should have about 8 cups. Whisk the sugar and cornstarch together in a large bowl, then add the plums. Drizzle with almond extract, then stir everything together. It will be a bit messy and clumpy, but don't worry.

4. Pile this mixture into the middle of the pastry and smooth it out, leaving a 2-inch border. Fold the pastry border up over the filling, pleating as necessary.

5. Bake 15 minutes. Reduce heat to 350°F and bake another 20 to 25 minutes or until the crust is golden and the filling is very bubbly. Let stand at least 1 hour before serving.

Tip For a golden top edge, brush the folded-over pastry with a little water or cream, then sprinkle it with coarse or granulated sugar before baking.

Make ahead The pastry can be made well in advance (see Tip page 251) and the pie can be baked and kept at room temperature for up to 12 hours.

Prep Time 15 minutes if pastry is made
Ready In about 2 hours

1 batch Forgiving Food Processor Pastry (page 251)

8 to 10 red plums

½ cup (105 g) granulated sugar

1 tablespoon cornstarch

1 teaspoon almond extract

Rhubarb and Apple Pie with Crumble Topping

Makes one 9-inch pie • Serves 8

Prep Time 20 minutes if pastry and topping are made
Ready In about 2 hours

1 batch Forgiving Food Processor Pastry (page 251)

Crumble Topping

½ cup (75 g) all-purpose flour

⅓ cup (40 g) quick oats

¼ cup (60 g) packed brown sugar

⅓ cup (85 g) butter, cold and cubed

Rhubarb and Apple Filling

5 thin stalks rhubarb, chopped (about 2 cups)

4 small apples, peeled, cored and sliced (about 2 cups)

¾ cup (155 g) granulated sugar

4 teaspoons cornstarch

⅛ teaspoon salt

Switch it up Use frozen rhubarb in place of fresh, but do not thaw it first. Increase the cornstarch to 5 teaspoons.

I rarely make double-crust pies. Instead, I've got a handful of shortcuts that are easier and more forgiving, and this crumble top is the best one of all—I get pie and crumble in one fabulous dish. Also, with a crumble top, much of the fruit's moisture evaporates during cooking, so you need less cornstarch in the fruit mix. This combination of rhubarb and apple is my dear dad's favourite, because the apple mellows the rhubarb's tartness without smothering it. This is essentially a fancier version of a fruit crumble, and I often make it for friends with spring birthdays. For this pie, I like Gala, Empire, Spartan or Granny Smith apples best because they don't disintegrate completely when cooked.

1. Preheat the oven to 425°F.

2. Roll out the pastry on a lightly floured counter, using a lightly floured rolling pin, into a 12-inch circle. Loosen the pastry from the counter by gently sliding a thin metal spatula underneath it, then transfer to a 9-inch pie plate. Gently press the pastry into the pie plate. There will be lots of over-hanging pastry.

3. Use scissors to clip off the excess pastry, leaving about 2 inches beyond the lip of the pie plate. Now fold the overhang in towards the centre so it's even with the lip of the dish. Using your fingers or a fork, crimp or pinch the folded edge to itself.

4. To make the Crumble Topping, stir the flour with oats and brown sugar in a large bowl. Add the butter and use your fingertips or a pastry blender to cut it into flour mixture until crumbly. Reserve.

5. To make the Rhubarb and Apple Filling, stir rhubarb and apples together in a large bowl. Stir the sugar, cornstarch and salt together in a small bowl, then pour over the fruit mixture. Stir well to combine. Scrape the fruit mixture into the pastry shell and gently smooth it into an even layer. Sprinkle evenly with Crumble Topping.

6. Place the dish on a baking sheet and bake for 45 minutes or until the pie is bubbly at the edges and the crumble top is golden. Let cool on a rack at least 45 minutes before serving.

Apple Crisp

Makes one 9-inch round or 8-inch square crisp • Serves 6 • Make ahead

This is the easiest dessert I know. Happily, it's also one of the best and well loved—and does it ever make the house smell good! The original recipe came from my grandma Ethel, whom I never really knew but whose handwriting is so familiar from recipe cards in my mom's collection. She would have made this by hand, but I whirl up the topping in the food processor to save a few minutes. Use any type of apple, such as Gala, Granny Smith or Honeycrisp, or a mix of what's in the fridge.

···

1. Preheat the oven to 375°F. Grease a 9-inch pie plate or 8-inch square baking dish with butter or non-stick cooking spray.

2. To make the topping, stir the brown sugar with the flour and cinnamon (if using) in a large bowl. Add the butter and use your fingers to squish the butter into the flour mixture. You should end up with some pea-sized lumps of butter, as well as some lima-bean-sized lumps.

3. Peel and slice the apples. Put the slices into a large bowl and add about ⅓ cup of the topping mixture. Stir well, then scrape the slices into the prepared baking dish, spreading them fairly evenly. Top with the rest of the topping and smooth it into an even layer.

4. Place the dish on a baking sheet, then bake 35 to 45 minutes or until the topping is golden brown and the filling is bubbly at the edges. Serve warm with ice cream, if desired.

Tip To make the topping in the food processor, whirl the brown sugar, flour and cinnamon first, then pulse in the butter.

Make ahead You can make the topping and freeze it in a resealable plastic bag for up to 1 month. You can also bake the crisp up to 1 day in advance and reheat it at 375°F for about 15 minutes.

Prep Time 20 minutes
Ready In about 1¼ hours

¾ cup (165 g) packed brown sugar

½ cup (75 g) all-purpose flour

½ teaspoon cinnamon (optional)

½ cup (115 g) butter, cold and cubed

6 medium apples

Rhubarb Crumble

Makes one 8-inch square crumble • Serves 4 to 6 • Make ahead

Prep Time 15 minutes
Ready In about 2 hours

Rhubarb Filling

1 cup (195 g) packed brown sugar

1 egg

2 tablespoons all-purpose flour

4 cups (475 g) chopped fresh rhubarb

Crumble Topping

⅔ cup (100 g) all-purpose flour

½ cup (55 g) quick oats

⅓ cup (65 g) packed brown sugar

⅓ cup (85 g) butter, cold and cubed

Crisp and crumble are two different desserts. Crisps have a topping made with just sugar, flour and butter, while a crumble's topping also contains oats (making it crumbly!). Both are members of the dessert family that also includes grunts, slumps, cobblers, buckles, brown bettys and pandowdies. The names are charming, but they're all just simple fruit desserts topped with some kind of buttery goodness. I prefer a crumble topping with rhubarb—it mellows the fruit's tart edge.

••

1. Preheat the oven to 375°F. Grease an 8-inch square baking dish, a pie plate or any medium baking dish with butter or non-stick cooking spray.

2. To make the Rhubarb Filling, whisk the brown sugar with the egg and flour in a large bowl. Stir in the rhubarb until well coated, then scrape the mixture into the prepared dish, spreading it into a fairly even layer. Wipe out the bowl.

3. To make the Crumble Topping, stir the flour with the oats and brown sugar in the same bowl. Add the butter and use your fingertips or a pastry blender to cut it into the flour mixture until crumbly.

4. Sprinkle the Crumble Topping evenly over the rhubarb. Place the dish on a baking sheet and bake 35 to 40 minutes or until bubbly and golden. Let it stand at least 45 minutes (or up to 12 hours) before serving. Serve with ice cream or whipped cream.

Tip If your garden (or your neighbour's garden!) gives you a bounty of fresh rhubarb, chop it into 1-inch pieces and freeze it in 2-cup batches.

Make ahead The crumble topping keeps well in the freezer for up to 1 month.

Switch it up You can use frozen rhubarb instead of fresh. Do not thaw it before baking, and add about 10 minutes to the baking time.

Lemon Custards

Makes eight 4-ounce ramekins • Make ahead

This recipe is so simple I'm always just slightly worried it won't work. Happily, it's perfect every time, and the result is a silky, intensely lemony pot of deliciousness that seems infinitely more complicated, and lives up to its fancy French name, *petits pôts de crème au citron*. It can be made well in advance, and the individual portions make it ideal for a dinner party (and since I rarely host more than six people, I always get a few extra custards for the next day).

Water-bath cooking may seem a little intimidating, but it's actually a rather forgiving way to make custards, since they're far less likely to overcook. I don't like to be left with unused egg whites: I never do this unless it's entirely worth it. This time, I promise you it's entirely worth it.

··

1. Preheat the oven to 300°F. Boil a kettle of water. Place eight ½-cup ramekins or cups in a deep roasting pan.

2. Zest 1 lemon, then juice all the lemons. Whisk zest and juice well with the sugar, egg and egg yolks. Whisk in the cream.

3. Strain the mixture through a sieve. Divide the strained mixture among ramekins. Place the roasting pan in the oven, then carefully add boiling water until it comes halfway up the sides of the ramekins.

4. Bake 40 to 45 minutes or until set but still slightly jiggly. Let cool in the water bath until room temperature, then take out of the water bath and chill at least 4 hours or up to 2 days.

5. Serve with whipped cream and raspberries, if desired.

Tip You can freeze the leftover egg whites for up to 3 months. Pour them into a resealable bag and squeeze out all the air. Label the bag with the quantity of egg whites. Thaw and use them in any recipe.

Make ahead Cover custards individually with plastic wrap and keep in the fridge for up to 2 days.

Prep Time 10 minutes
Ready In about 5 hours

3 lemons

1 cup (205 g) granulated sugar

1 egg

6 egg yolks

1¾ cups whipping (35%) cream

For serving

Whipped cream

Raspberries

Date-Coconut Squares

Makes 16 squares • Make ahead

Prep Time 20 minutes or less
Ready In about 2 hours

1 package (13 ounces/375 g) pitted dates (about 2½ cups)

1 cup water

Zest of 1 lemon

2 tablespoons fresh lemon juice

1¼ cups (185 g) all-purpose flour

1 cup (195 g) packed brown sugar

¼ teaspoon baking soda

2 cups (220 g) quick oats

½ cup (50 g) unsweetened shredded coconut

1 cup (225 g) butter, cold

Make ahead Cool cooked squares completely, then wrap unsliced squares first in foil, then in plastic wrap. Freeze in a large resealable plastic bag for up to 1 month. Thaw, still wrapped, at room temperature before cutting.

Date squares are like the devilled eggs of the sweet world: homely but universally adored. They were a staple on dessert tables of my youth—at church fairs, bake sales, family parties and funerals. Mom called them "matrimonial cake," which I never understood since date squares hardly seem pretty enough for a wedding. There's no need to splurge on expensive Medjool dates for this recipe. Since they will be boiled and flavoured, the block of dates you find in the baking aisle are perfect (and what I always use). The worst part of my recipe used to be chopping up the block of dates, so one day I skipped that step, and it works out just as well! The classic doesn't call for coconut, but after making these, you'll wonder why.

1. Preheat the oven to 375°F. Grease an 8-inch square baking dish with non-stick cooking spray or butter. Line with a piece of parchment paper, leaving an overhang on two sides.

2. Combine the brick of dates with water in a small pot. Cover and bring to a boil, then reduce heat and simmer gently, covered, for 5 minutes or until the brick is soft enough to break apart. Stir well, then simmer, covered, another 5 minutes or until the dates are very soft. Stir well again. The pot should be fairly dry and the dates very pasty. If not, cook another 2 to 3 minutes. Remove from the heat and stir in the lemon zest and juice.

3. Stir the flour, brown sugar and baking soda together in a large bowl. Stir in the oats and coconut. Using the large holes of a box grater, grate the butter right into the oat mixture. Stir until each flake of butter is well coated with oat mixture.

4. Transfer about half of this mixture (about 3½ cups/425 g) to the prepared dish. Press it firmly and evenly into the dish. Top with the date mixture, spreading it evenly. Sprinkle evenly with remaining oat mixture.

5. Bake 45 to 50 minutes or until golden. Let cool completely on a rack, then gently pull upwards on the overhanging parchment to remove the square from the dish. Cut into 16 pieces.

Tip You can make the crumble in a food processor instead of by hand. Whirl flour, brown sugar and baking soda until well combined. Add oats and coconut and pulse two or three times, until just combined. Cut butter into cubes, add to the food processor and pulse several times, or until mixture forms coarse crumbs.

One-Pot Chocolate-Pecan Brownies

Makes 16 brownies • Make ahead

When we were kids, my mom often made rich, fudgy brownies from *Joy of Cooking*. She doled them out in tiny one-inch squares, and my brother, sister and I loved them passionately. So imagine my delight when I saw big four-inch-square brownies in bakeries—they seemed enormous! I quickly learned that they're too big for me, though. I prefer to make intensely flavourful, rich, satisfying brownies eaten in just a couple of bites.

I've been tinkering with this recipe for years, always trying to use as few bowls as possible, and getting the balance of chocolate, sugar, eggs and flour just right. It may seem strange that there is neither baking powder nor soda here, but don't worry—their absence makes the brownies even more dense and indulgent.

··

1. Preheat the oven to 350°F. Spray an 8-inch square baking dish with non-stick baking spray (see page 4).

2. Melt the chocolate and butter together in a medium pot over low heat. Stir in the sugar until it has mostly dissolved, about 3 minutes. Remove from the heat and let cool 10 minutes.

3. Add the eggs, vanilla and coffee powder (if using) to the pot and whisk to combine. Add the flour and salt and stir well, making sure to get into the edges of the pot. Stir in the pecans and chocolate chips until just combined.

4. Scrape the batter into the prepared dish. Bake 30 to 35 minutes or until the top is firm and a cake tester comes out almost but not fully clean—these are fudgy brownies, so it should still look a bit damp. Let cool in the dish on a rack 10 minutes, then flip out of the dish to cool completely.

Make ahead These last well for up to 3 days, wrapped with lots of plastic wrap and kept at room temperature.

Switch it up The nuts and chocolate chips are optional and changeable. Replace with the same quantity of any chopped toasted nut, white chocolate chips, peanut butter chips, butterscotch nibs or dried fruit.

Prep Time 15 minutes
Ready In about 1 hour

4 squares (4 ounces/115 g) unsweetened chocolate

¾ cup (180 g) butter

1¼ cups (260 g) granulated sugar

3 eggs

2 teaspoons pure vanilla extract

1 teaspoon instant coffee powder (optional)

1 cup (150 g) all-purpose flour

⅛ teaspoon salt

1 cup (100 g) chopped toasted pecans

½ cup (90 g) semi-sweet or dark chocolate chips

Strawberry and Lime Buttermilk Muffins

Makes 12 muffins • Make ahead • Batch cooking

Prep Time 15 minutes
Ready In about 45 minutes

1 cup (150 g) all-purpose flour

¾ cup (105 g) whole wheat flour

¾ teaspoon baking powder

½ teaspoon baking soda

¼ teaspoon salt

¾ cup (155 g) granulated sugar

1 egg

2 teaspoons pure vanilla extract

Zest of 2 limes

⅓ cup (85 g) butter, melted

¾ cup buttermilk, shaken before measuring

1 cup strawberries, diced into ½-inch pieces

2 to 3 small strawberries, thinly sliced (optional)

Lime Glaze

1 tablespoon fresh lime juice

⅓ cup (30 g) icing sugar

Switch it up You can use almost any fresh, sweet fruit in place of strawberries. Try raspberries, blueberries or chopped peaches, pears or nectarines.

This is one of the most popular recipes I've ever written. I developed this gem because I couldn't find an amazing muffin recipe anywhere else, and its popularity proves my point: everyone loves muffins because they're fun and easy to make, but there aren't many great recipes out there. They're usually too fatty, too sweet or—when the pendulum swings back—too grainy and dry. Real buttermilk was the key to cracking the muffin code; it makes these muffins so fluffy and tender. I love the tangy lime glaze, but you can skip it if you prefer.

1. Preheat the oven to 400°F. Line a muffin tin with paper liners, or grease well with non-stick baking spray (see page 4).

2. Whisk all-purpose and whole wheat flours with baking powder, baking soda and salt in a large bowl. In a separate medium bowl, whisk sugar with egg, vanilla and lime zest until well combined. Whisk in butter, then buttermilk. Add liquid mixture to flour mixture. Using a rubber spatula, stir until just combined.

3. Before mixture is fully incorporated, add strawberries and stir just three or four more times or until barely combined. Immediately spoon or scoop into the prepared tin. Top each muffin with a slice of strawberry, if using.

4. Bake 5 minutes. Reduce heat to 350°F and bake another 20 to 25 minutes or until tops are golden and a cake tester inserted into the centre of a muffin comes out clean. Let muffins cool in the pan for 10 minutes.

5. To make the Lime Glaze, add lime juice to icing sugar in a small bowl and stir well. Transfer muffins to a rack. Drizzle with Lime Glaze, then cool completely.

Tip Although you can mix milk with vinegar as a substitute for buttermilk, I highly recommend using real buttermilk here. Its consistency and tanginess can't be replicated. If you're worried about having extra buttermilk you won't use, try my Buttermilk Waffles (page 17).

Make ahead Glazed muffins keep well, in an airtight container or resealable plastic bag at room temperature, for up to 3 days.

Batch cooking Freeze cooled, unglazed muffins in resealable plastic bags for up to 10 days. Thaw in the bag at room temperature. Drizzle with glaze when fully thawed.

Banana Bread

Makes one 9- x 5-inch loaf • Serves 10 to 12 • Make ahead

Life just isn't complete without banana bread. The majority of people must agree with me, because it's consistently one of the most-searched recipes on the internet. And although you can certainly add chocolate chips or nuts to this recipe, I'm partial to the plain version, in which the banana takes centre stage (with a little boost from the lemon zest). This is truly a bread and not a cake because it's less sweet than many versions you find at coffee shops. You can increase the sugar to 1 cup if you prefer.

When bananas get too brown for eating, tuck them into a resealable plastic bag and store in the freezer. When it's time to bake, simply thaw and peel; the bananas will be brown and liquidy—perfect for this recipe (use the brown liquid too!). Don't use non-fat yogurt here; you need some dairy fat to help the yogurt do its thing.

....

1. Preheat the oven to 350°F. Generously grease a 9- x 5-inch loaf pan with non-stick baking spray (see page 4).

2. Stir the flour with the baking soda and salt in a large bowl. In a separate large bowl, whisk the brown sugar with the butter. Whisk in the eggs, bananas, yogurt, vanilla, and lemon zest and juice. Scrape the banana mixture into the flour mixture and stir to just combine.

3. Scrape the batter into the prepared pan. Bake 55 to 65 minutes or until a cake tester poked into the middle of the loaf comes out clean. Let cool in the pan 10 minutes, then turn out onto a rack to cool completely.

Make ahead Wrap the cooled loaf in foil and place in a resealable plastic bag. Freeze for up to 1 month. Sometimes I slice it first before freezing; this way, if I'm having a midday sweet craving I can thaw one slice just for me.

Switch it up Add 1 cup of chocolate chips, chopped walnuts or unsweetened coconut (or ⅓ cup of each, if you want to add all three ingredients) to the butter mixture before combining it with the flour mixture.

Prep Time 20 minutes
Ready In a little over 1 hour

2 cups (300 g) all-purpose flour

¾ teaspoon baking soda

½ teaspoon salt

¾ cup (165 g) packed brown sugar

½ cup (115 g) butter, melted

2 eggs

3 very ripe bananas, mashed

½ cup plain yogurt

2 teaspoons pure vanilla extract

Zest of 1 lemon

2 tablespoons fresh lemon juice

Grown-Up Ice Cream Sundaes

Makes 6 sundaes • Make ahead

Prep Time 10 minutes
Ready In about 10 minutes

¾ cup whipping (35%) cream

1 teaspoon instant coffee powder

3½ ounces (100 g) milk chocolate, chopped (about ⅔ cup chopped)

3½ ounces (100 g) dark chocolate, chopped (about ⅔ cup chopped)

6 cups (1½ L) best-quality coffee or vanilla ice cream

2 tablespoons single-malt Scotch

Flaky sea salt, such as Maldon

Ice cream is everyone's fall-back dessert, the one we serve when there's no time to bake. But if you have just a few more minutes, you can easily make chocolate ganache to pour all over it, thus turning ice cream into something fancy. To increase the sophistication, I make this deliberately not kid-friendly and add all the things kids can't, won't or shouldn't consume—Scotch, coffee, dark chocolate and flaky salt. Not only do these ingredients make the dish complex and delicious, but they also make it feel more thoughtful and special.

I use Scotch because it's what we love and have on hand in my house, but you can substitute any best-quality spirits you like, from bourbon or brandy to Baileys or Kahlúa.

1. Combine the cream and coffee powder in a small pot and heat over medium-high heat until just barely simmering. Add the chocolate, turn off the heat and stir until the chocolate is melted and the sauce is smooth.

2. Prepare 6 bowls of ice cream. Drizzle each portion of ice cream with 1 teaspoon Scotch, then with some chocolate sauce. Sprinkle with a pinch of salt.

Make ahead Make the chocolate sauce and keep refrigerated for up to 2 days. Reheat gently on the stove or in 30-second increments in the microwave, stirring between each increment.

Acknowledgements

I'm indebted to many friends, old and new, who helped create this book by inspiring, supporting and encouraging me. I owe every one of you a killer dinner.

Andrea Magyar, my editor, who believed in me before this book was even an idea. Andrea has a magic touch with cookbooks, and it's been an honour to be one of her writers and to benefit from her guidance.

Photographers Alyssa Wodabek and Chris Sue-Chu, food stylists Melanie Stuparyk and Lindsay Guscott and prop stylist Catherine Doherty: the artists who brought my recipes to life. They understood my vision for the book even better than I did, and looking at the images still makes me well up with pride.

My recipe testers, a team of over 100 volunteer home cooks who cooked and evaluated every recipe in the book. Their questions and feedback made these recipes immeasurably better, and their enthusiasm made the process of creating this book even more fun.

The fierce, funny women who helped me, hugged me and harassed me (depending on the day): Karma Brown, Alison Fryer, Karyn Gordon, Beth Hitchcock, Jenny Kingsley, Ceri Marsh, Zoe Maslow, Tracy Moore, Michelle Pennock, Sasha Seymour, Mairlyn Smith, Carol Toller, Heather Trim, Aimée Wimbush-Bourque, and honorary girlfriends Ethan Adeland, Joel MacCharles, Chris Nuttall-Smith and Bruce Sellery.

My Cityline family, who always have my back, and who let me be my silly, bad-dancing, messy self.

My Food Bloggers of Canada clan, particularly our secret society of self-doubting cookbook authors, who gave me advice, answers or just virtual hugs at any hour of the day.

Lucy Waverman, Maria Charvat, Lynda Reeves and Jane Francisco, my mentors and former bosses, who showed me how to be smart and strong, and what it means to be a boss in every sense of the word.

My neighbours Lisa, Olivia, Margot and Elissa, who graciously accepted doorstep deliveries of cakes with a slice out and casseroles missing one portion, and poured me large glasses of wine in return.

Margaret, Brian, Dylan and Erin Tansey, my food-loving family, who taught me everything in life, from the importance of good bread to the healing power of a martini. Their love and support is the foundation of everything I do.

Michael, who enthusiastically eats everything I cook, supports me in all of life's ups and downs and always makes me laugh. And Thomas, who delights us every day, and who is so fun that I can't actually accomplish any work while he's around. These boys fill every one of my days with joy and love.

And my best friend Katie Dupuis, the Cyn to my Tess, who coaches me through any crisis and celebrates every success. Katie held my hand through each step of this journey, read (and tweaked) every word of this book, and helped me chill out just ever so slightly.

Thank you.

Index